The Social Thought of
Georg Simmel

Social Thinkers Series

Series Editor
A. Javier Treviño
Wheaton College, Norton, MA

Published
The Social Thought of Georg Simmel
By Horst J. Helle

The Social Thought of Émile Durkheim
By Alexander Riley

The Social Thought of C. Wright Mills
By A. Javier Treviño

Forthcoming
The Social Thought of Karl Marx
By Justin P. Holt

The Social Thought of Erving Goffman
By Michael Hviid Jacobsen and Søren Kristiansen

The Social Thought of Talcott Parsons
By Helmut Staubmann

The Social Thought of
Georg Simmel

Horst J. Helle
University of Munich, Germany

Los Angeles | London | New Delhi
Singapore | Washington DC

Los Angeles | London | New Delhi
Singapore | Washington DC

FOR INFORMATION:

SAGE Publications, Inc.
2455 Teller Road
Thousand Oaks, California 91320
E-mail: order@sagepub.com

SAGE Publications Ltd.
1 Oliver's Yard
55 City Road
London EC1Y 1SP
United Kingdom

SAGE Publications India Pvt. Ltd.
B 1/I 1 Mohan Cooperative Industrial Area
Mathura Road, New Delhi 110 044
India

SAGE Publications Asia-Pacific Pte. Ltd.
3 Church Street
#10-04 Samsung Hub
Singapore 049483

Printed in the United States of America.

Library of Congress Cataloging-in-Publication Data

Helle, Horst Jürgen.

The social thought of Georg Simmel / Horst J. Helle, University of Munich, Germany.

pages cm.—(Social thinkers series)
Includes bibliographical references and index.

ISBN 978-1-4129-9765-2 (alk. paper)

1. Simmel, Georg, 1858–1918. 2. Sociology—Philosophy. I. Title.

HM479.S55H444 2015
301.01—dc23   2013037526

This book is printed on acid-free paper.

Acquisitions Editor: Jeff Lasser
Editorial Assistant: Lauren Johnson
Production Editor: David C. Felts
Copy Editor: Diana Breti
Typesetter: C&M Digitals (P) Ltd.
Proofreader: Annie Lubinsky
Cover Designer: Gail Buschman
Marketing Manager: Erica DeLuca

Certified Chain of Custody
Promoting Sustainable Forestry
www.sfiprogram.org
SFI-01268

SFI label applies to text stock

14 15 16 17 18 10 9 8 7 6 5 4 3 2 1

Contents

Series Editor's Foreword

The SAGE Social Thinkers series is dedicated to making available compact, reader-friendly paperbacks that examine the thought of major figures from within and beyond sociology. The books in this series provide concise introductions to the work, life, and influences of the most prominent social thinkers. Written in an accessible and provocative prose, these books are designed for advanced undergraduate and graduate students of sociology, politics, economics, and social philosophy, as well as for scholars and socially curious general readers.

The first few volumes in the series are devoted to the "classical" thinkers—Karl Marx, Emile Durkheim, Max Weber, Georg Simmel, George Hebert Mead, Talcott Parsons, and C. Wright Mills—who, through their seminal writings, laid the foundation for much of current social thought. Subsequent books will feature more "contemporary" scholars as well as those not yet adequately represented in the canon: Jane Addams, Charlotte Perkins Gilman, Harold Garfinkel, Norbert Elias, Jean Baudrillard, and Pierre Bourdieu. Particular attention is paid to those aspects of the social thinker's personal background and intellectual influences that most impacted his or her approach to better understanding individuals and society.

Consistent with SAGE's distinguished track record of publishing high-quality textbooks in sociology, the carefully assembled volumes in the Social Thinkers series are authored by respected scholars committed to disseminating the discipline's rich heritage of social thought and to helping students comprehend key concepts. The information offered in these books will be invaluable for making sense of the complexities of contemporary social life and various issues that have become central concerns of the human condition: inequality, social order, social control, deviance, the social self, rationality, reflexivity, and so on.

These books in the series can be used as self-contained volumes or in conjunction with textbooks in sociological theory. Each volume concludes with a Further Readings chapter intended to facilitate additional study and research. As a collection, the Social Thinkers series will stand as a testament to the robustness of contemporary social thought. Our hope is that these books on the great social thinkers will give students a deeper understanding of modern and postmodern Western social thought and encourage them to engage in sociological dialogue.

Premised on Newton's aphorism, "If I have seen farther, it is by standing on the shoulders of giants" (an aphorism, incidentally, that was introduced into sociology by Robert K. Merton, himself a towering figure in the discipline), the Social Thinkers series aims to place its readers on the shoulders of the giants of 19th- and 20th-century social thought.

Acknowledgments

The following pages are dedicated to the women and men who want to understand how culture and society change. Among them are my former students and my colleagues who challenged me over the years with their questions and with the role model they gave me. More recently, I was asked to lecture about Simmel in China. There, the role model decidedly included the students whose interest in and knowledge of the history, philosophy, and sociology of "The West" repeatedly made me feel ashamed about how little I know about the 5,000 years of Chinese culture and history: Chinese intellectuals know so much more about us Westerners than we know about them. Continuing this trend, they wanted to study Simmel.

Simmel was way ahead of his time in realizing that the world is becoming more and more unified. Increasingly, what must have appeared visionary in his days has become a reality. The Simmel scholars who, in a wider sense, were my teachers were typically marginal men who did not depend on translations to read Simmel. Kurt Wolff, Reinhard Bendix, Everett C. Hughes, and Herbert Blumer were among them. This book is published in their memory and as a grateful acknowledgment of their scholarship, wisdom, and kindness.

Introduction

Why Study Simmel?

Simmel's Concern for Change

Sharing with his contemporaries a concern about the ambivalent impact of change in culture and society, Georg Simmel tried to understand the complexities of industrialized and modernized social life. He confronted such problems as inequality, social order, social control, deviance, the social self, rationality, and reflexivity, and he was interested in a new and wider approach to **alienation.** In this context, he also encouraged a developmental approach to ethics. Simmel devoted his work to the problems of

1. Devising, experimenting with, and applying a method for the study of cultural change;

2. Exploring the scope of human creativity as dealing with degrees of freedom in society; and

3. Delineating the limits of freedom and establishing reasonable rules for restrictions.

Simmel studied issues of personality and the development of the individual in his or her life course. Although personality is often explained as dependent in part on **social structure,** Simmel sees it more in its interplay with culture and developments like advancements in religions and other worldviews. He imposes the duty on individuals to recognize and pursue their unique "calling" and to acquire the knowledge and abilities needed to reach that goal. All human beings live under the severe duty of becoming what they are destined to be. That, of course, includes the responsibility to acquire as high a level of education as possible. The looming threat of bureaucratization and the power relations it produces is treated by Simmel as an aspect of alienation (i.e., that something loses its original beneficial purpose and starts leading a dubious life of its own). He deals with the topic of money as a special case of the general phenomenon of alienation.

Simmel is a champion of **individualization** on the basis of a refined consciousness, of an awareness of the unique potential and of the "calling" of the person. To him, the most striking worldwide trend leading to change in ethics is progressive individualization. But while there is this interest in change, he respects the continuity of **cultural evolution** and does not believe in sudden jumps and breaches in history. Accordingly, the primary interest of Simmel's social thought with regard to the dynamics implicit in the human condition is not *revolution* but *evolution*. That interest, indeed, leads to the demand for more knowledge and education.

There is no coherent theoretical framework that would identify Simmel's thinking because he shrinks from letting any constructions of ideas become self-serving and thereby alienated from the purpose of devising novel contributions to social thought. Instead, he emphasizes as a central topic in his reflections the moral responsibility of each modern individual to consider the social, personal, and historical dimension of people's lives. Thus, while *The Social Thought of Georg Simmel* cannot be presented as a system composed of a list of specific terms to be memorized by the student, it can nevertheless be demonstrated in its application to social problems. That shall be done in this text with reference to social change in ethics, religion, family life, and the economy. These and other areas of social development will be discussed as illustrations for the need to devise a dynamic approach to culture and society.

In his **interpretive sociology**, Simmel presents a balanced approach toward the unavoidable tension between individual and society under modern global conditions. On the one hand, he sees society as a system of positions into which individuals must be taught to fit, like one prepares to be qualified for a certain occupation. But in society in general this occurs on a much wider scale than in the labor market. People must learn to act like a woman or a man respectively, like a young person or an elderly person, like a person in a teaching position or one in a learning position, and so on.

This simplified notion is complicated by at least two additional considerations: (1) Each individual must learn to simultaneously fit into a number of such positions by being, for instance, a male, a young adult, a student, and a sports coach at the same time; and (2) the emphasis on cultivating one's unique potential as an individual shifts the attention away somewhat from wanting to fit into a given position in society. This will be dealt with in more detail later.

Summary of the Chapters

This text presents to the reader the social thought of Georg Simmel in eight chapters, as follows: It is the purpose of Chapter 1 to familiarize the student of Simmel's work with the historical and cultural context in which it was conceived and published. The chapter introduces Simmel as teacher and writer. A trained philosopher, he founded sociology as one of the humanities rather than letting physics and biology be the sources of inspiration for a method. He had a successful Jewish merchant as his father, and he was influenced by the fact that the generation of his parents left the Jewish faith to become Christians.

Simmel valued frankness and truthfulness higher than diplomacy, which caused him considerable troubles in his degree processes at Berlin University. His informal influence can only be guessed from the fact that his home was the meeting point for prominent personages of the Berlin intellectual and cultural scene, including Max Weber. His students included George Herbert Mead, Robert E. Park, Max Scheler, and Martin Buber. They, in turn, have taught such giants in sociology as Shmuel Noah Eisenstadt in Israel and Fei Xiaotong in China. His legacy includes drawing conclusions from Darwin's insights for the humanities that make it the duty also for sociologists to think in dynamic categories and to develop better theories of social and cultural evolution.

Simmel's work unfolds against this personal and substantive background. One of its typical traits is the inclination to look for qualities of relationships. At the same time, society is a central topic for him, and he states that society consists of a sum of interactions. In the course of such interactions, reality is socially constructed. It follows from this construction process that competing views of reality result and that there are alternative perspectives from which social reality as a whole can be looked at. Dealing with emotions is a crucial topic in Simmel's social thought. Emotions influence what we do and even what we perceive as real. Finally, Simmel takes on naïve notions about such crucial political concepts as liberty and equality and writes that to tell people that liberty and equality can be developed in politics as a friction-free alignment of the two is simply an opportunistic lie.

Chapter 2 is devoted primarily to Simmel's method. He describes the prevalence of the natural sciences over the humanities because the former promised progress and better living conditions. But he does not want to see the sciences become the sole source of orientation. Since in the history of **Western civilization** the split between arts and sciences could not be reconciled, Simmel places sociology on the side of the humanities.

Sociology is needed because large social groups like classes take over from exceptional individuals the initiative in social change. It is sociology's primary task to develop new ways of looking at things and thus to apply an unfamiliar approach to a familiar problem in the study of society. Society is possible for three reasons: (1) Individuals are generalized into categories of people, (2) a person's integration into society always leaves out some aspects due to the uniqueness of him or her, and (3) the collectivity demands that each member is different so he or she can find his or her special place in society compatible with his or her individuality.

Chapter 3 deals with the structure of society and with instructions directed to persons on how to conduct themselves. The latter are usually referred to as *social norms*. Simmel sees change on both levels of analysis: The structure opens up, allowing us to live in wider company; the norms are adjusted to this evolution by following the idea for a **dynamic ethics**. These changes are the requirements to be met in order to enable individualization as the decisive trait of **modernization**. To recognize and develop to the fullest his or her innate potential is, to Simmel, a central task for the modern person. Fulfillment of this task hinges on the courage of the individual to be different to the point of becoming a **stranger**.

Systems of ethics can be distinguished by either emphasizing brotherly closeness among all humans (**universalism**) or else stressing the superiority of a certain group of people (**exclusivity**). Universalism as a program may result in changes to make the world more peaceful; as an established condition, however, it frequently lacks tolerance for strangeness and leads to stable, but potentially rigid, conditions. Exclusivity, on the other hand, encourages strangeness and accordingly promotes innovation. Individuals may be reluctant to live the lives of innovators for two reasons: (1) fear of losing the approval of friends and other persons close to them, and (2) fear of loss of identity. Many of the great innovators had to endure persecution and exile. They are remembered today for their courage as well as their contribution to cultural evolution.

In Chapter 4, the sociologist of religion finds a definition suitable for this particular academic field of research: Religion is a system of beliefs that defines life after death as real. It is not within the scope and ability of sociology to determine whether religious statements about the beyond relate to anything that exists. This question must be left open. However, to the believer and follower of a religion, the statements of faith must be true, must relate to something real, and must be based on personal relationships with one or several immortal persons that are eternal; he or she cannot be religious unless all of these are experienced as fact.

The discoveries of modern sciences cannot be blamed for the weaknesses in religious faith in recent times. But the way of thinking that comes with science leads to defining as believable reality only what can be proven in a laboratory experiment. Simmel asks how the acceptance of religion can be restored. He suggests that the established religions leave their respective transcendental worlds of ideas and observe the unique impulses of life itself. Simmel thinks intellectual development can rob religion of its clothing, but it cannot take religion's life: A new **form** will be found for religiosity because it is one of life's basic **contents.**

Chapter 5 presents Simmel's ideas on private life and on women. Research findings from cultural anthropology and comparative family studies have shown that a variety of **family types** exist, but what they all have in common, in Simmel's view, is the mother-child dyad as their center. Biological fatherhood is seen by him as a late development in the evolution of culture. It became important only at the time when material goods were handed down to the next generation according to blood relationship. Simmel sees monogamy as having an evolutionary advantage because it produces a better educational situation for the offspring than other family types do.

Simmel explains changes following his rule of reversal: At first marriage arrangements made by family members precede romantic love; then, that is reversed. At first the need for offspring leads to marriage; later people get married and then decide to have children. In less-developed cultures, the groom pays a price to gain his wife; later the fact that the wife has been the result of major sacrifices raises her value in the eyes of her husband. Simmel also looks at the division of labor between genders, first on the individual level between one woman and one man, then on the group level between all women and all men of one society as the two gender groups confront each other, and finally on the division of labor within the group of women: Some of them become academics; others are left behind.

Finally, in this chapter Simmel explains why the demise of the patriarchal household is unavoidable. Then he describes the uniqueness of marriage in comparison to all the other dyads. It is based on the quality of special closeness in married life, on the role of the "third person," and on the contradiction between individual freedom and collective control. On the one hand, a couple experiences the privacy of its marital life as free from social interference, but on the other hand, the community will intervene immediately in cases of marital offenses or child abuse. Simmel describes the psychological conditions of jealousy and gives relationships beset by this emotion little chance of recovery.

Chapter 6 deals with competition and with money. Conflict is necessary to promote evolution, and competition is desirable because it is an indirect way of fighting and because it occurs to the benefit of other people. Governments have the duty to defend competition. A precondition for competition to function well is equality of chances in the market. Simmel points out that equality and liberty cannot be reconciled; rather, they turn out to be alternatives. Simmel compares the cry for equality to a pair of crutches on which the demand for liberty came limping into history.

Money is, to Simmel, the most powerful illustration of the **social construction of reality**. Its value is ascribed to it, but due to alienation, that definition process is not acknowledged. The value of money originates in exchange situations: Goods to be given one for the other in a barter economy tend to be of different value. As their exchange is negotiated, their value relation is abstracted from the two goods in question and counted as units of money. Money is, accordingly, an expression of the interdependence of people; it is the most general form of a social relationship.

In Chapter 7, Simmel's ideas about the **poor person** and about life are combined. Being poor is looked at as the quality of a relationship. Taking care of poor persons is placed by Simmel in the duality of rights and duties: The same action, like supporting a poor person, can be seen as the right of one and the duty of another. Because large groups of dissatisfied poor persons are perceived as potential hotbeds of political unrest, governments develop welfare programs. The considered purpose of those is to keep the poor person inside society.

Simmel sees life in the context of his **evolutionary theory**. The life of humankind as it has unfolded over millennia is reflected in the lives of individuals. To predict the path culture and society will take in the future, it is not realistic to rely on human reason alone. Collective emotions will play a significant part in evolution. Emotions are personal, and to curb them from having bad effects Simmel recommends distancing interests from persons. In the foreseeable future, it may become difficult to keep primary hopes in sight. Instead, there will be a multitude of tools required to achieve one's goals. As a result, people may lose sight of what they wanted those tools for in the first place. Chapter 8 introduces as further reading Simmel's well-known lecture on mental life in the metropolis, about the impact living in a big city has on cultural change.

1

Georg Simmel

The Man and His Work

Personal Background

Georg Simmel was a much sought-after public speaker and very well-liked college teacher. Some senior colleagues were jealous of him because of his popularity among students as a fascinating lecturer. Some of his most notable texts (on the metropolis, on competition, on money, on conflict in modern culture) were originally delivered as public addresses before a nonacademic audience. After sociology had already established itself as a positivist **physics of the social,** as defined by its early founder **Auguste Comte** in France, and after in Germany **Wilhelm Dilthey** had spelled out why the Comtian type of sociology was, to him, a dead-end alley of scholarship, Simmel reinvented sociology within the domain of the **humanities,** with close ties to history, philosophy, and ethics; however, it was too late to change the ugly name "sociology" that Comte had invented as a replacement for "physics of the social." Simmel created his vision of sociology as one of the humanities (more on this in Chapter 2).

In Simmel's lifetime, in the Germany of the 19th century, the humanities were represented by capable philosophers and historians and were accordingly well developed there. Being a philosopher by training, Simmel placed the new discipline side by side with philosophy, ethics, history, humanistic psychology, and cultural anthropology. In the United States, until the 1960s, many university departments combined sociology and cultural anthropology (e.g., Department of Sociology and Anthropology).

Simmel's initiative triggered considerable international attention: Two famous contemporaries, only slightly younger than Simmel, undertook the journey to Berlin to listen to his lectures. George Herbert Mead (1863–1931) spent time as a doctoral candidate at Simmel's university. Robert E. Park (1864–1944) traveled there with his wife and three children to study with Simmel. He arrived in the fall of 1899 (Raushenbush, 1979, p. 30). The name of the university was not Humboldt University, as it is today, but rather Friedrich-Wilhelms-Universität, named after the German emperor (Simmel, 1881, title page).

Park took notes of Simmel's lectures in 1899, to make them available to his students at the University of Chicago, where both Mead and Park later taught for decades. Mead (1901) was one of the first scholars to write a review of Simmel's (1907) mammoth book on money within months of Simmel's work becoming available. And Park (together with his colleague Ernest W. Burgess) started a new school of sociology in Chicago, following Simmel's ideas. Simmel's life tragically ended at the close of World War I as the result of an insurmountable health problem. But his legacy as a social thinker is getting more and more attention and increasing in momentum, as shown by recent publications about his work.

Simmel was of Jewish origin. His father had become a Catholic. Simmel himself belonged to a Protestant church. He grew up the youngest of seven children and received a sizable inheritance after the death of his father. This financial independence meant he could afford to be intellectually free and did not have to follow schools of thought that may have been current in academic circles at the time: In addition to having enough money, it was not compatible with his personality to behave in an opportunistic way. His frankness and sincerity frequently caused friction, even while he was undergoing academic examinations, as we shall see here later.

With the exception of the last four years, when he became a professor in Strasbourg, Simmel spent his life in Berlin. In 1876, when he was 18 years old, he became a freshman at the university known today as Humboldt-Universität zu Berlin. He was a student there for five years. He majored in philosophy, and his teacher introduced him to the works of Kant, Hegel, Schopenhauer, and Nietzsche. It appears that of these, Kant had a lasting and decisive influence on him (Simmel, 1881, p. 33; Tenbruck, 1958, p. 588).

In 1881, Simmel submitted his doctoral thesis, hoping to quickly receive the degree of doctor of philosophy (abbreviated in Austria, Germany, and Switzerland as *Dr. phil.*). But his dissertation dealt with the evolutionary history of music, citing Charles Darwin as a central figure in his research. The evaluators rejected the dissertation because of what they referred to as "patchwork-like sketchiness" and "insufficient precision of the line of reasoning." Nevertheless, Simmel succeeded in publishing his work after converting his text into a journal article (see Simmel, 1882). But clever as it may have been of Simmel not to throw away his manuscript, publishing it in a journal still did not give him a doctoral degree.

It seems that although his professors—at least some of them—disliked his study on the history of music, they did not dislike the man Simmel. Therefore they suggested he submit another manuscript he wrote that had won a prize in a competition. Simmel may have been shy to use the same work for two separate purposes, but that reservation was overcome by the encouragement he received from his academic teachers. Thus he handed in as his doctoral thesis a manuscript that he had written outside his university ambitions. In this manuscript he dealt not with Darwin, but rather with Kant, which indeed resulted in his getting the degree. In the list of Simmel's publications, it appears as his first book (Simmel, 1881).

In Germany in Simmel's time, and even to this day, it is expected that a future professor will write yet another book after his doctoral dissertation, called *Habilitationsschrift*. According to that rule, two years after receiving his doctoral degree, Simmel handed in to the same faculty of philosophy at the University of Berlin another manuscript on the philosophy of Kant. This time, the successful completion of the graduation process would lead to the license to teach philosophy independently, that is, without any controlling supervision by another university teacher. The title that comes with that license is *Privatdozent*.

Simmel again, as in the case of getting his doctorate, eventually succeeded, but this time the process was even more unusual. Again, the thesis was turned down, but then Professor Dilthey vigorously came to Simmel's defense and persuaded his reluctant colleagues to accept it. During Simmel's oral defense of his thesis, a truly dramatic event occurred: Professor Zeller remarked that he considered a specific lobe of the brain to be the seat of the human soul. Simmel entirely ignored the situation he was in and without hesitation declared Zeller's point of view to be nonsense. Even though some of the faculty members most likely agreed with him, his behavior was unacceptable, and as an immediate consequence, Simmel did not pass this examination on his first try (Schnabel, 1976, p. 273).

The circumstances that accompanied Simmel's doctoral and postdoctoral examinations were probably remembered among the philosophy professors of the university for a long time. In addition, in the literature about his life, frequently anti-Semitism is mentioned as a likely reason for his career difficulties. In spite of all the various impediments, in January of 1885 Simmel passed the postdoctoral examinations in philosophy and was appointed a *Privatdozent* at the philosophical faculty of the University of Berlin.

Because he was a wealthy man, he did not depend on the money he was making by teaching. He and his wife Gertrud lived in a comfortable house, and his contemporaries described his lifestyle as follows: Simmel used to work in the mornings and evenings, but he preferred to see guests and friends in the afternoons. His closest friend was the professor of economics Ignaz Jastrow, with whom Simmel frequently discussed the topic of money. Both talked in such a manner that the one hardly listened to what the other said; despite this, they always had the impression of having understood each other well. (During the early years of my tenure at the University of Munich, a professor of economics who was very much senior to me told me that he was a former student of Jastrow's in Berlin. He confirmed Jastrow's style of oral communication.) In any case, Simmel learned about the perspective on money then current in economic theory firsthand from an expert in that field.

Overall, the life Simmel led in Berlin appears to have been peaceful and successful. He must have been an extraordinary teacher: For his lectures, he carried almost no notes to class and improvised as he talked. Also, he wrote his articles for journals or newspapers one after the other, without second drafts or corrections, as if he already could see them take form in front of his mind's eye (Gassen & Landmann, 1958, p. 13). Most likely, these conditions and characteristic resulted in the admiration of some and the jealousy of others.

In 1898, the faculty to which he had belonged as *Privatdozent* since 1885 requested that he be given a tenured position as an associate professor (*professor extraordinarius*; see, however, Coser, 1968). The Ministry of Cultural Affairs did not grant this request. In February 1900, the same academic body repeated its attempt to make Georg Simmel a professor extraordinarius. This time the appointment was granted. From there on he received a regular salary. Thus Simmel spent virtually his entire career below the rank of full professor. Only during the last four years of his life was he a full professor at the University of Strasbourg. Those four years were not happy years because he missed the cultural challenges of Berlin and anticipated the outcome of World War I.

During his long, pleasant and socially highly fruitful years in Berlin, Simmel and his wife Gertrud succeeded in making their household a cultural center. Great names in scholarship and art were regular guests of the Simmels, such as Rainer Maria Rilke, Stefan George, Edmund Husserl, Reinhold and Sabine Lepsius, Heinrick Rickert, Max and Marianne Weber, and others.

Close to the end of his life, Simmel was faced with the diagnosis of an incurable disease. He asked his doctor, "How long do I still have to live?" He needed to know because an important book still had to be finished. The doctor told him the truth, and Simmel used the weeks left to him to complete his last work: *Lebensanschauung* (Perspectives on Life). On September 26, 1918, Simmel died from cancer of the liver in Strasburg. Many sources erroneously name September 28 as the day of his death because that was the date on the coroner's report (Becher, 1984). Death at this point in time "was perhaps a blessing because many former Strasbourg professors fell into utter poverty shortly thereafter, when Alsace became French again" as a result of the outcome of World War I (Gassen & Landmann, 1958, p. 13).

Intellectual Influences

The great intellectual movements of lasting consequences in Simmel's days are linked with the names of Charles Darwin (1809–1882), Karl Marx (1818–1883), and Sigmund Freud (1856–1939). It is noteworthy that Darwin and Marx were contemporaries and that their lives overlapped considerably with that of Freud. Like most other intellectuals who lived in 19th-century Germany, Simmel explicitly confronted the works of Darwin and Marx. As has been mentioned before, Simmel's failed first attempt at submitting a doctoral thesis was tied to the ideas of Darwin. Simmel (1905) criticized an aspect of the work of Marx in the second edition of his *Die Probleme der Geschichtsphilosophie* (The Problems of the Philosophy of History), a text that Max Weber (1864–1920) refers to as the most convincing source available at the time for studying the method of interpretive sociology (Weber, 1951).

As a philosopher by training, Simmel was well familiar with **ancient Greek philosophy,** but also with the Germans Kant, Schopenhauer, and Nietzsche. Kant was admired as well as criticized by Simmel. Admiration resulted from Kant's insight that we cannot produce an image of reality without building our own preconceived ideas into the product we create. Reality is, therefore, always the result of a construction process: If we want to understand the way certain people see certain things, we must try to reconstruct the process in the course of which they arrived at their specific image of reality.

Regardless of this admiration, Kant was criticized by Simmel on account of his egalitarian ideas. Kant proposed the ethical principle that our conduct ought to be guided by rules that can be generalized for all human beings (a principle commonly referred to as *categorical imperative*). Simmel, by contrast, asks, "Can I not demand more of myself than of the average fellow citizen? Can I therefore not impose more stringent rules upon myself than upon others?" So while Kant's egalitarian ethic is designed to prevent people from finding any extra easy way out for themselves, it also prevents them from performing above average. The latter is precisely what Simmel was not willing to accept. His familiarity with the writings of Kant is documented in his officially accepted doctoral dissertation (Simmel, 1881), in his published lecture course on Kant (Simmel, 1924), and in his comparison of Kant's philosophy with that of Goethe (Simmel 1913, 1916).

In addition to Simmel's indebtedness to Kant, Darwin's new insights had a significant impact on Simmel's method, an impact that cannot simply be sorted into the controversy between evolutionism and creationism. What matters to Simmel about Darwin's contribution is the notion of change, the awareness of movement, which he hoped would replace the perception of petrified social conditions so prevalent in 19th-century Germany. Accordingly, his primary question is not whether God is at work in his creation, nor is it whether humans are responsible for social evolution or whether there is nothing they can do about it because automatic processes dictated by natural law have taken over. Important as these issues may be, Simmel's primary question is this: May we assume that our concept of an ideal society, our notions of exemplary conduct, our basic rules of ethics, will still be the same for our grandchildren as they have been for our grandparents? His answer obviously is, No! But it is not that simple.

The notion of movement over time applied to culture and society as well. According to what Simmel learned from Darwin, evolution was not a concept reserved for biology and geology. Therefore, Simmel asks, could it be that there is a development toward even better conditions of human existence? This leads him to the exciting and very unpopular idea that a dynamic concept of a future ethic might not only be theoretically possible but even politically desirable. This conviction is the background for his *Einleitung in die Moralwissenschaft* (Introduction to the Moral Science; Simmel 1892, 1893), a two-volume critique of fundamental concepts of static ethics that was highly controversial from the day it was published.

Darwin

Darwin's explanation of the origin of species was seen by many as merely a contribution to biology. But to Simmel it changed philosophy; it changed the notion of personal development; it changed our whole way of thinking—or, in any case, it should. Instead of viewing the tiger, the dog, the elm tree, and the human being as fixed and constant for all times, Simmel felt that Darwin compelled him to think of all those concepts as fluid. At the end of his famous book *The Origin of Species* (1859), Darwin concluded that "there is grandeur in this view of life, with its several powers, having been originally breathed into a few forms or into one; and that, whilst this planet has gone cycling on according to the fixed law of gravity, from so simple a beginning endless forms most beautiful and most wonderful have been, and are being, evolved." No anti-religion activist would write about life "having been originally breathed into a few forms."

This quote from Darwin is admittedly open to various interpretations, but it must be taken into consideration by anyone with an open mind. What interested Simmel in this text was the fact that Darwin combined the idea of the earth *moving* around the sun, the geological layers *moving* up and down (sometimes causing earthquakes), and the plants and animals *evolving*. All this together resulted in a new concept of development, independent of the question whether God created this world in seven days, or in seven years, or in seven million years. Simmel did not ask Darwin whether or not it was God who created the world; Simmel wanted to know whether God created a world that changes or a world that does not change, and the conclusion Simmel drew in his social thought is obvious: It changes!

Simmel's Influence on Others

When we rightfully deplore the tragic and devastating effects of wars, we usually think about loss of lives and destruction of houses, bridges, and other infrastructure. What we frequently do not think about are the long-lasting effects on culture, knowledge, and scholarship. Simmel's popularity in Europe and the United States was virtually cut off by World War I. Many of his former students and admirers could not continue their academic careers as sociologists. Before the damage World War I had caused could even be assessed, the horrors of the Hitler regime and of World War II added to the destruction of intellectual culture in Germany and Europe and, as a consequence, led to a gross neglect of Simmel's legacy in the thirties and forties virtually everywhere.

In spite of these catastrophic conditions, the torch that Simmel had lit was carried on. When Robert E. Park retired from the University of Chicago in 1936, he went to China to teach there. The way Park presented sociology included what he had learned from Simmel in Berlin. About Park's remarkable stay in Germany, we learn the following:

> In the spring of 1900 he took three courses with Georg Simmel who was then forty-one and a docent in the university. The courses were in "Ethics," "History of Philosophy in the Nineteenth Century," and "Sociology." This was the only course in sociology Park took in his entire life. Years later Park was to say that Simmel was "the greatest of all sociologists." (Raushenbush, 1979, p. 30)

Park's (1928) well-known journal article on the Marginal Man is a modified version of Simmel's concept of the Stranger.

As has been mentioned above, in 1936 Park went to China. He taught at the missionary-founded Yenching University in Peking, which had China's best sociology program at the time. Among his students was Fei Xiaotong (or Fei Hsiao-Tung, 1910–2005). Fei was a pioneering researcher and professor of sociology and anthropology; he was also well-known for his studies on China's ethnic groups and was a social activist. Many of the influential sociology professors in China today are his former students (Shen, 2001). Through Fei as mediator, many of Simmel's concepts were passed on to become the way sociology is practiced in contemporary China.

While Simmel taught at the University of Berlin, he had an audience that was remarkably international for the time. Among his students were Mead and Park from America, as I mentioned above. In addition, there were young intellectuals from Eastern European countries, particularly from Poland and the Czech Republic. How much of Simmel's influence is at work there today as a result of these contacts remains to be researched. Considerable similarities in the work of Simmel and Florian Znaniecki from Poland (Helle, 2000) have been documented in publications of the Polish sociologist Elzbieta Halas.

One of Simmel's most influential students was Martin Buber (1878–1965), who was 20 years younger than Simmel. Buber was

> predominantly dedicated to three areas: the philosophical articulation of the dialogic principle (*das dialogische Prinzip*), the revival of religious consciousness among the Jews (by means of the literary retelling of Hasidic tales and an innovative German translation of the Bible), and to the realization of this consciousness through the Zionist movement. (Zank, 2008)

Buber lectured at Frankfurt University and at "the university he had helped to create—the Hebrew University of Jerusalem" (Zank, 2008).

In Jerusalem, Martin Buber became an important academic teacher of Shmuel Noah Eisenstadt (1923–2010; Eisenstadt, personal communication). In 1947, Eisenstadt received his doctorate in sociology at the Hebrew University with Buber as his chief adviser. Looking at Simmel's influence on others, we thus have at least these two lines of intellectual descent, the line Simmel-Park-Fei leading to China and the line Simmel-Buber-Eisenstadt leading to Israel. Pointing to these "lineages" is obviously a simplification of how Simmel's ideas were passed on because Fei's legacy is not limited to China and neither is Eisenstadt's limited to Israel.

In Germany, Max Scheler (1874–1928) went to Berlin from his native Munich to study with Simmel and Wilhelm Dilthey. In 1910, Leopold von

Wiese (1876–1969) published a review article summarizing the then-current publications in sociological theory in *Archiv für Sozialwissenschaft und Sozialpolitik* (von Wiese, 1910). In his overview about the different approaches to social thought, von Wiese places Simmel's (1908/2009) groundbreaking book into context and gives it the recognition it deserved but later failed to receive. In 1919, von Wiese started teaching at the University of Cologne, where he held the first professorship in sociology that was ever established in Germany. He wielded considerable influence as a result of founding the journal *Kölner Vierteljahreshefte für Sozialwissenschaften* (Cologne Sociological Quarterly), which still exists today as *Kölner Zeitschrift für Soziologie und Sozialpsychologie* (Cologne Journal of Sociology and Social Psychology). Von Wiese wanted to follow Simmel, whose influence can also be traced to Hans Freyer in Germany. Freyer was the head of the Leipzig School, which was informed by the work of Scheler. That school is associated with Freyer's student Arnold Gehlen and, in turn, Gehlen's assistant Helmut Schelsky (Üner, 1992).

In the United States, excerpts from Simmel's (1892, 1893) two-volume book *Einleitung in die Moralwissenschaft* (Introduction to the Moral Science) were published in the *International Journal of Ethics* very soon after it appeared in German. Also, the chapter "The Problem of Sociology" in his book *Sociology* (1908/2009) was previously published in *Annals of the American Academy of Political and Social Sciences* (1895a). This, plus what was mentioned here before about the influence of Robert Park, shows that Simmel was known in America during his lifetime.

A decade after the end of World War II, in 1955, The Free Press, then located in Glencoe, Illinois, published a book with translations of texts by Simmel. The book was titled *Conflict & The Web of Group-Affiliations*, translated by Kurt H. Wolff and Reinhard Bendix. In the foreword to that volume, Everett C. Hughes thanks Wolff for doing "American scholars a distinct service by translating and publishing important parts of the sociological work of Georg Simmel in a volume entitled *The Sociology of Georg Simmel* (1950)" (Simmel, 1955, p. 7). Hughes then also expresses his gratitude to Reinhard Bendix for "making an additional chapter of Simmel's *Soziologie* available." Hughes travelled to Germany in the late fifties and was able to participate in seminar discussions there because his German was fluent. In his foreword to the Simmel book, he regrets that "Americans whose mother tongue is English (including those among them whose mother tongue was not English) are extremely loathe to learn other languages" (p. 7). Hughes was an American who had studied German as part of the language requirements for getting a doctorate while both Wolff and Bendix, who emigrated from Germany, were German native speakers.

Other contributors to 20th-century social thought, such as Peter L. Berger, who moved to America from Austria, and Erving Goffman (1922–1982), who moved to the United States from Canada, have acknowledged their indebtedness to Simmel in their publications. So did Anselm L. Strauss (1916–1996). In addition, Americans who have contributed to spreading Simmel's ideas and making him better understood by scholars and students who read English include Peter Etzkorn, Guy Oakes, Donald Levine, Deena Weinstein, and Michael A. Weinstein. On the influence of Simmel's work in the United States, see also the article by Levine, Carter, and Mills Gorman (1976).

During his lifetime (1858–1918), Simmel observed the social, economic, and political changes that occurred: The transition of Prussia and, under its leadership, of Germany from a predominantly agrarian to an industrialized country; the rise of capitalism all over Europe; the unification of the German-speaking territories, with the exception of Austria and Northern Switzerland, into the Second Empire in 1871; and the downfall of Germany as an empire with colonies at the end of World War I. Simmel's thinking became, in part, a reflection of these changes, of the economic advances, the horrors of war, the ambivalence of life in the metropolis, and the political intolerance throughout the nation. His ideas are inspirations today to create fresh interpretations of similar events from the perspective of a humanist approach to social thought. In light of these vast challenges, Simmel was convinced that sociology could supply moral guidance and had the relentless duty to do so.

Simmel's Work: Looking for Qualities of Relationships

What sociology ought to stay focused on are *relationships*. The problems to be studied by sociologists are located not *inside* persons but *between* them. That is what makes social reality a significant topic: Being social means being oriented toward relationships. An example will help illustrate that: A violent gang of youthful males may puzzle the adults in charge of supervision because group members, if interviewed individually, appear to be peaceful and well-behaved adolescents. No inclination toward violence can be detected in any one of them as an individual person. One will therefore have to conclude that the qualities typical of the group as a whole are peculiar to this association of persons. They cannot be assessed by simply adding the characteristics of its members. The whole then (in this case, the group) is more than—or in any case different from—the sum of its components.

That is a familiar formula in social philosophy. However, Simmel develops this insight further. He looks at **qualities of relationships** in a more general context. To him, reality is not merely inherent in the person, with what goes on between persons simply to be deduced from who and how they are; instead, relationships have a primary reality of their own, not to be derived from anything else. His take helps explain the above observation, that group qualities cannot fully be deduced from characteristic of individual members. His emphasis on the quality of relationships also explains the topics of his research and publications: Simmel describes, for instance, the stranger not as a person representing strangeness but as a participant in a strange relationship; he describes the poor person not as someone belonging to a statistical category with a low income but as someone who is dealt with by others as being poor.

Obviously, there is also the objective reality of having not enough money to buy food or pay the rent, and thus there is the grim fact of being poor, no matter how people look at it. It is typical for Simmel that he would not see in that observation a rejection of his view but an alternative way of looking at the problem of poverty. Each of the two perspectives on the poor person may be justified, depending on the specific condition under sociological investigation as well as on the intention for action the observer may have or lack. The stranger and the poor are illustrations of Simmel's sociology as the study of *qualities of relationships.*

To Simmel, what really matters is—as we have seen—what goes on between people: Someone wrote these lines and you read them, so this book "goes on" between the writer and the reader. Someone talks and somebody else listens, so what is spoken "goes on" between the two. Money is spent by one person and another person cashes it in. And, indeed, Simmel's interest in money is based on that. So, what matters to Simmel as his primary reality is what goes on between people. It is not *this* person's unique abilities or *that* person's characteristic moods; rather, it is the special quality of the relationship between two or more persons. Sociology, as Simmel wanted to initiate it, was then going to be *the study of the quality of relationships* as fundamental social realities.

As we have seen, the lines we read, a book we study, sentences spoken to us, a song we listen to, and even money we spend can be dealt with as existing *between* persons. Obviously, the subject of erotic love falls within Simmel's interest as well. In that context, one can research narcissism as a condition describing the love someone feels for himself or herself. But also, in that case Simmel would describe narcissism as an attitude the individual takes toward himself or herself, as if even then the object were another person, although in fact it is merely a different aspect of the same narcissistic individual. So in this case too, if we stretch things somewhat, we are dealing with the quality of a relationship. Simmel looks at the law, too, as the quality of a relationship: The way one person treats another person may be legal or illegal and thereby give their interaction the respective quality. Thus, whether the law will be abided by or broken can also be looked at as the quality of a relationship. Indeed, literature, music, art in general, money, love, and law are Simmel's topics precisely because they can be looked at as qualities of relationships.

Society as a Topic

Obviously, in addition to studying relationships, sociology is also concerned with society as a topic. That is consistent with what has been explained here so far because to Simmel, society is the sum of all relationships that potentially influence each other. He writes in his text on competition: "Society . . . is nothing but a sum of interactions" (Simmel, 1903b, p. 1010). This definition makes it plausible that today we are dealing with a global society because what happens in one part of the world may influence peoples in other parts. Under modern global conditions, potentially everybody is interacting with everybody else worldwide. And society—whether seen as local, national, or global—changes, develops, or decays due to progress, wars, and catastrophes, but still, in spite of all that to a remarkable degree, society maintains itself and perseveres in an established way.

Stability as well as change can be observed in history because a society consists of relationships between living persons. Some societies in history remain stable; others develop and change over time. There is some "division of labor" according to which one segment of the population may be bent on keeping established traditions alive, while another segment concentrates on changing things. To this day, political parties tend to emphasize tradition on the one hand or demand change and development on the other. In their own way, these segments may each contribute to keeping the society going.

Any new development in how people interact in a given society must preserve the unique characteristic of the history of culture. In order to be able to even describe change, one has to be dealing with a phenomenon that retains its identity, for otherwise it would not be possible to state what it is that changed. Instead, one would have to acknowledge that one phenomenon has been replaced by another. Because of this condition, continuity and change depend on each other, and even a conservative and a liberal political party depend on cooperating inside the society they share.

And although Simmel's topics appear to be quite diverse, he consistently deals with a few very fundamental questions that will recur in most of the chapters that follow here.

- How is society possible?
- How can society be studied?

- How does society change?
- How can human beings know what to do?
- How can sociology be useful?

This will be explained in more detail in Chapter 2.

The Social Construction of Reality

Simmel wrote explicitly on music and published texts devoted to such masters as Dante, Michelangelo (as a poet), Goethe, Rembrandt, and Rodin. It is important to note, however, that he did not, as it were, compartmentalize social reality into segments that could then be labeled as religion, academic institutions, art, and so on. Rather, he identified those areas as alternative perspectives from which *social reality as a whole* can be looked at. Thus there is a religious construction of reality, a scholarly construction of reality, and an aesthetic construction of reality. Those constructions do not interfere with each other: To Simmel, there was as little potential for conflict between them as in art between colors and tones.

Simmel perceived these constructions as conflict-free alternative re-creations, and just as it would be ludicrous to claim a conflict between a poet's, a painter's, and a composer's rendering of the same theme, he could not understand how religion and science could possibly be in conflict. To Simmel, they merely find themselves dealing with the same subject matter, each from his own specific perspective. The origin of life and the world is basically just as inconceivable for the faithful as for the scientist. However, they do—and, according to Simmel, they should—take the liberty to socially construct an explanation from their cherished perspective. But often, as a result, what had thus been constructed then—alas—passes as the ultimate answer to a question that cannot really be answered fully by anyone.

With these basic methodological tools, Simmel goes to work on very special problems. He writes on the stranger whose strangeness is socially created in interaction; on the metropolis as a modern interactive context of city life; on money and socialism as alternative means for dealing with modernization (He who has money does not need socialism). He writes on the **secret** as an indispensible means for distinguishing between people who are close and others who are distant. He writes on the poor person as key to understanding a network of duties and obligations in interaction. Simmel's flexibility in method is typical for his writing. He uses alternative approaches to his social theory, not because his conceptual decisions are presented haphazardly but because different ways of looking at the world are merely tools for him to use, in the hope to get as close as possible to the *real thing*.

For instance, the mood I am in is the *real thing*, but there is no way for anyone, including myself, to capture it directly. In order to approach it indirectly, I need to describe how I feel, using language, maybe supported by facial expressions, gestures, and mimicking as tools. Then my relatives and friends who are exposed to my mood can voice criticism on two levels: They may not like the mood I am in, or they may not like the way I describe it to them, or, of course, both. Or, to take a different example: If I go to church and find myself disillusioned by the sermon, that may be because of its message as content or because of the form in which it was delivered, or again, because of both. This distinction between the deep-seated, often emotional reality that is always difficult to access and the tools used in communicating it is typical for Simmel. It is hard to imagine how anyone can do research on the family, on religion, or on art without making this distinction.

Dealing with **emotions** is a crucial topic in the social thought of Simmel. Different qualities are typically attributed to a relationship according to the emotional needs of the attributor. If I need to get rid of my anger, I will attribute an antagonistic quality to the relationship in which I participate at the time. If I am inclined to fall in love, I may attribute a loving quality to my partner. This leads Simmel to the topic of alienation, meaning the denial of authorship and responsibility.

The relationship becomes *alien*, or unfamiliar to me, because I will not admit that it was I who carried a particular quality into the relationship. Small children always argue that *the other* child started the fight. I will argue that I fell in love because *the other* person is indeed lovable, not because I was in need of that emotional makeup. And again, as in the case of dealing with the subject of poverty, there is in addition the more neutral perspective of objective facts: Just as the poor person may *really* have nothing to eat, the person I fell in love with may *really* be incredibly attractive.

Liberty and Equality

Simmel debates what goes on between people in various ways, also looking at how they deal with secrets they want some contemporaries to know about while hiding them from others. Not only do we attribute qualities to relationships according to our current emotional needs, we also make distinctions between our different social ties according to the information we share. The person closest to us knows everything about us because we tell him or her everything. The greater the distance, the more we withhold knowledge from others because the information is "none of their business." Accordingly, we distinguish by distance and are unable and unwilling to treat all our contacts equally.

This notion presupposes, of course, that what we keep a secret is not necessarily information about some type of immoral activity. The busybody who wants to tell everything to everybody may succeed in making himself or herself "much in the news" but at the price of being unable to differentiate between people close to him or her on the one hand and more distant persons on the other. Against this background, Simmel refutes the widespread opinion that one should not have any secrets. To him, having secrets is a prerequisite for managing the distances at which we want—and need—to keep this or that fellow human.

As a consequence, having secrets promotes inequality. To certain traditions of political thinking, **equality** has a very high value. The free press as principle of information management is of fundamental importance for political equality in a democracy. Simmel's defense of the secret can, therefore, be read also as the rejection of journalistic intrusion into a person's private life. There is in Simmel's writings the Socratic question: What do you mean by equality? Do you mean uniformity, as in China in the days of Mao's Cultural Revolution? Do you mean sameness, as in refraining from making distinctions between male and female, old and young? Or do you mean *equal dignity and value* in spite of the obvious difference between individuals? It is highly significant to clarify that.

Simmel reminds us that the French Revolution erroneously suggested it could introduce the simultaneous realization of liberty, equality, and fraternity. Although the implementation of fraternity in a society is a topic that would lead us too far afield at this point because it would have to be discussed in the context of early Christianity as well as that of utopian communism, Simmel makes the striking remark that liberty and equality are incompatible. He argues that we either have equality without liberty, as in socialism, or we have liberty without equality, as in liberalism (Simmel, 1949).

To tell people that liberty and equality can be developed in politics as a friction-free alignment of the two is simply an opportunistic lie. Simmel compares the cry for equality to a pair of crutches on which the demand for liberty came limping into history. Once liberty has established itself, it can throw away those crutches because it now stands on its own strong legs. Equality is now no longer needed.

Conclusion

It is the purpose of this chapter to familiarize the student of Simmel's work with the historical and cultural context in which it was conceived and published. The chapter introduced Simmel as teacher and writer. A trained philosopher, he founded sociology as one of the humanities rather than letting physics and biology be the sources of inspiration for a method. His father was a successful Jewish merchant, and Simmel was influenced by the fact that the generation of his parents left the Jewish faith to become Christians.

Simmel valued frankness and truthfulness higher than diplomacy, which caused him considerable troubles in his degree processes at Berlin University. His informal influence can only be guessed from the fact that his home was a meeting point for prominent personages of the Berlin intellectual and cultural scene. Max Weber was among them as a regular guest. Simmel's students include Mead, Park, Scheler, and Buber. They, in turn, have taught such giants in sociology as Eisenstadt in Israel and Fei in China. Simmel's legacy includes drawing conclusions from Darwin's evolutionary insights for the humanities that make it the duty also for sociologists to think in dynamic categories and to develop better theories of social and cultural development.

Simmel's work unfolds against this personal and substantive background. One of its typical traits is the inclination to look for qualities of relationships. At the same time, society is a central topic for him, and he states that society consists of a sum of interactions. In the course of such interactions, reality is socially constructed. It follows from this construction process that competing views of reality result and that there are alternative perspectives from which social reality as a whole can be looked at. Dealing with emotions is a crucial topic in Simmel's social thought. Emotions influence what we do and even what we perceive as real. Finally, Simmel takes on naïve notions about such crucial political concepts as liberty and equality and writes that to tell people that liberty and equality can be developed in politics as a friction-free alignment of the two is simply an opportunistic lie.

Looking back at this first chapter may give rise to a few questions:

- What was peculiar about teaching philosophy and sociology at the University of Berlin at the time Simmel was there?
- How could Simmel's pioneering work have impacted the early stages of sociology worldwide?
- What is the significance of the notion of reality as being socially constructed, and why did that idea stay alive in the history of sociology?
- Was it old-fashioned or far-sighted of Simmel to include the impact of emotions in his social thought, and why?

2

Sociology as One
of the Humanities

Is Sociology a "Science"?

Simmel did his research, teaching, and publishing in Germany at a time when that country was undergoing rapid development from a traditionalist agrarian region to a modern industrial nation. Industry as the production of large numbers of identical items at a conveyor belt in big cities was seen then as the successful application of the natural sciences in modern technology. The sciences, therefore, were popular because putting research results into practice appeared to guarantee increasingly higher standards of living.

In his lecture on the metropolis, Simmel (1903a) saw a connection between thinking in the categories of the natural sciences and dealing with money in the economy:

> Modern mind has become more and more calculating. The calculative exactness of practical life which the money economy has brought about corresponds to the ideal of natural science: to transform the world into an arithmetic problem *(Rechenexempel)*, to fix every part of the world by mathematical formulas. (Simmel, 1903a/1950, p. 3)

The sciences found popular support and were widely preferred over the humanities for yet another reason. As can be observed in totalitarian countries to this day, research in philosophy, history, and certainly sociology often leads to insights that clash with the intentions of the political and religious leadership. Because of that, sociology was forbidden in Hitler's Germany as well as in other dictatorial regimes. Generally speaking, in the history of scholarship there has been a better chance in the natural sciences than in the humanities to keep political as well as religious interference out of the academic discourse.

Looking at it this way, the discoveries of Darwin did not present a problem for the sciences. The findings of Darwin appeared so political from the start not because of their implications for biology and geology but because those findings suggested—at least to Simmel—the need to develop a new method in the humanities.

Simmel complained that during his lifetime, the influence of the natural sciences on culture and society was beginning to be oppressive. In his opening arguments of the original version of his text on Kant and Goethe (Simmel, 1906, 1916), he describes the situation as it evolved out of the findings of Galileo and Copernicus, who presented the shocking insight that the earth was not the center of the universe. Those two initiated, most likely against their will, the development of a worldview that reduces reality to rigid cause and effect: What forces the individual parts to integrate into one whole is not a will or an idea but pressure, push, and the attraction of gravity kept in balance, hopefully, by centrifugal power. The earth does not fall into the sun because it revolves around it fast enough. But it should also not increase its speed because then the earth would take off into space, eventually leaving our solar system. In summary, then, our world is governed by natural laws that can be expressed in mathematical formulas. Simmel finds this explanation of our existence to be most disconcerting, should it ever become the only one available to us.

If what happens in this world is merely the result of natural law, then it can be likened to a clockwork running mechanically (Simmel, 1906, p. 2). But worse than an old-fashioned clock, it does not even represent ideas and purposes conceived by humans. Simmel saw the principle of the natural sciences to be in opposition to everything that, in the past, had given *meaning* to the world. The sciences are admirable and they are badly needed for progress and for improving human living conditions, but to use them as the sole source of interpreting the world, and thus to make them the foundations of a modern worldview, appeared to Simmel to be an alarming trend. It would, if continued unchecked, leave "no room for ideas, values, purposes, for religious meaning and for the freedom of ethical choice" (p. 2). The conclusion to be drawn from these reflections obviously cannot be to condemn the natural sciences, or to propagate a superiority of the humanities in the construction of a worldview; rather, the preferred consequence must be the acknowledgment that every effort should be made to restore unity between the arts and the sciences.

Simmel was convinced that the human mind, the person's emotional makeup, and the orientation toward traditional metaphysics were sufficiently strong motives that placed before the great thinkers of the 17th and particularly the 18th century the task to restore the lost unity between the arts and the sciences on a higher level (Simmel, 1916, p. 10). Simmel introduced Kant and Goethe into his writing as two giants in world literature who contributed to that goal more than almost anyone else. Both the philosopher Kant and the poet Goethe undertake in their work the task to restore the unity between the natural sciences on the one hand and the humanities, like philosophy, history, and sociology, on the other.

However, his project of making humanities and sciences coworkers in understanding the world has failed. Simmel's fear that they would work against rather than with each other has become more and more justified. Faced with the confrontation between the two camps of scholarship, Wilhelm Dilthey (1833–1911) argued that sociology belongs to the humanities. He pointed out that the objects under study in any one of the natural sciences—the molecule or a living cell, for instance—are not endowed with a conscious mind and therefore cannot be treated as subjects of their own decision making; nor can they be treated as participating in the process of the social construction of reality. A human being, by contrast, under study in the humanities, does have a consciousness and therefore should not be treated as a thing but as an individual with personal freedom as its prime characteristic.

Simmel followed Dilthey in the conclusion that sciences and humanities devote their efforts to objects so vastly different from each other it would be irresponsible to try to use the same method in both spheres of scholarship (Helle, 2013, p. 5). The method applied must fit the task at hand and—perhaps more important—must be compatible with the particular object under study. Therefore, sciences and humanities ought to work each within its own specific method.

In addition, the process of dealing with conflicting opinions is markedly different in the camp of the sciences as compared to the humanities. Disagreements in the natural sciences usually lead to proclaiming that one side is in error. In the humanities, on the other hand, the result of a difference of opinion may be an intensification of dialogue directed toward finding common ground: The same content permits two or more alternative perspectives from which to approach it. In the sciences, results of research are required to be much more independent of the perspective from which they are examined.

We can add the following to the reasons why Simmel sees sociology in the camp of the arts rather than in that of the sciences: Outside the academic world—and frequently even inside—the sociologist deals with creations of the minds of persons who are not scholars and whose thinking is not disciplined by rules of scholarship. It is the sociologist's task, nevertheless, to study and understand those creations. The natural scientist—ideally—does not have that problem.

The social reality of culture and society, as it is in and of itself, cannot be recognized; humans must rely on the construction of images and concepts to gain insights. But then they often claim what they have socially constructed is, in fact, reality. (Consider, for example, the claim "The Bible is the word of God." In English, in French, in Latin? Which is God's language?) In the humanities, this leads to the question, "Under which condition do people think things are real?" In sociology, what humans perceive as real depends on the perspective from which they look at things; a pessimist sees more bad things than an optimist. The method used is a tool, not a truth in itself. Just as we do not drive a nail into the wall with a screwdriver but with a hammer, the tool must be appropriate for approaching the particular topic. Accordingly, the methods of the natural sciences have limited use for sociology.

Simmel, therefore, set out to develop a method for the study of culture, art, religion, human emotions, the family, and similar areas of interaction. Other topics in sociology may be studied with other methods. In contrast with other founders of sociology, Simmel did not see sociologists as followers of physics, biology, or the natural sciences in general. Instead, he wanted sociology to be a field in the humanities as a neighbor of philosophy, history, and humanist psychology. Simmel is the founder of interpretive sociology, which is also called *verstehen* or humanistic sociology. (Humanistic, in this context, refers to an approach to education that uses a focus on the humanities to inform students.)

What Is Sociology?

Simmel was critical of people who see sociology as the universal discipline of human affairs. Doing that would make it a catch-all for anything social, with no distinct borders, like a newly discovered territory in which every homeless or uprooted area of research can stake a claim. The fact that human thought and actions occur in the context of society was, to Simmel, not a sufficient and acceptable reason for dealing with every aspect of it in a sociological context. He also rejected any definition of sociology as a collective term for the accumulation of certain facts, empty generalizations, and abstractions. If sociology is to establish itself as a serious and respectable discipline, it must differentiate itself within the broad field of the social sciences, which includes economics, psychology, and history. It must be in a position to emphasize the distinctiveness of its approach.

Simmel wrote about what he thought sociology ought to be in his article "The Problem of Sociology." That text was to be the first chapter of his 1908 book (Simmel, 1908/2009). There he explained how sociology came about during the 19th century as a reaction to the political power of the masses that established themselves against the interests of the individual. Overcoming the individualistic approach to history required giving up the traditional manner of conducting intellectual enquiry into social processes. The method of ascribing all important phenomena to the action of commanding individuals had come to an end.

Crucial events were no longer seen merely as the result of the willpower and ingenuity of Alexander the Great, or of Charlemagne, or of George Washington. A new understanding was beginning to find acceptance that saw the forces of social developments as being rooted in society and in social classes, rather than in this or that person. The new discipline of sociology, Simmel believed, attempted to take account of this. Simmel gives these examples: art, religion, economic life, morality, technological progress, politics, and health. They all are areas in which, he believed, people were beginning to realize that society was not only the target, but also the originator of movements and events.

At first glance, this justification of sociology as the study of social forces appears to contradict Simmel's emphasis on individualization as a process toward uniqueness of the person. But there are two separate levels of analysis that must be distinguished: In the study of social development as it occurs in history, attention shifts from the individual political, religious, or military leader to pluralities of people such as elites, classes, and masses, whereas in the study of personal development as result of education and socialization in families and schools, attention shifts toward fostering the unique abilities of the irreplaceable male or female person.

Simmel turned to describing what he wanted to constitute sociology and what he wanted sociology to be. Although all the humanities have to acknowledge that humans are influenced by the fact that they live in interaction with each other, sociology differs from them not by *what* is under investigation but by *how* it is studied. Sociology, then, was to Simmel a new method, a novel approach that would help investigate familiar phenomena from an unfamiliar angle. For sociology to establish itself as an independent new discipline, it had to raise the concept of society to the level of an overarching idea to which other phenomena would then have to be subordinated. By being viewed in the context of society, and to the extent to which that happened, they all were to become the object of one discipline, sociology.

What Is Society?

What people do together was seen by Simmel as the interactions they engage in. Because they interact, individuals influence each other and plan future activities in a certain context, like a college campus or an urban community. The widest context in which the actors relate to each other is society. Society consists of the sum of the interactions that occur in it. It is real, rather than merely an abstract concept in the minds of certain people. This is derived from the thesis that reality is embodied in relations. And it is, indeed, the interactions between individuals that constitute life itself. The reality with which social science is therefore concerned does not only consist of an accumulation of isolated persons who are, as it were, anatomically dissected, lifeless entities; instead, we are to perceive life as a unified whole, integrated into society through interaction.

The central concept that identifies sociology as a discipline is thus *society*. This all-encompassing idea, too, has the familiar two aspects: society as content and society as form. Society as content is the mass of people who compose it and who, of course, have a reality beyond the social. To study what is content, however, is not the task of sociology. Other disciplines, like history, psychology, statistics, or economics, are responsible for that. Sociology, then, is the study of society as form, as the highest and overarching form that encompasses all the other forms within it.

Sociology asks, "In which forms do persons relate to each other?" Form and content do not signify separate *objects* but distinct *aspects* of what sociology studies. Simmel called **contents** those driving forces that move individual persons to interact, but which by themselves are not yet social. Examples include impulses, interests, inclinations, and psychological conditions of a person that cause humans to turn toward one another. Other illustrations of content are hunger, love, and religiosity.

Forms come about as a result of the interaction motivated by these contents. Individuals create together, and for each other, social forms in the context of which their wishes can be fulfilled, their desires can be realized, their behavior can become traditional and reliable. The forms are based on a common interest of people to work together on a long-term basis, like a church that serves religious needs or marriage that serves erotic needs. All forms culminate, so to speak, in the form at the highest level, which is society. The chapters that follow Chapter 1 in Simmel's (1908/2009) book *Soziologie* are illustrations of the variety of forms in society.

Simmel points out that identical forms can come about in society on the basis of totally different contents, therefore serving quite disparate purposes from a functional perspective. We encounter, for instance, the civilized form of conflict called "competition" as the ordered physical exercise in a sports competition, in academia as the ambition to publish more than a colleague, or as the attempt to make a better impression on a father among siblings in a family. Competition is here the common *form* of conduct, but the *contents* are diverse as physical performance, excellence in scholarship, and family love.

On the other hand, Simmel also wanted his readers to understand that identical content may produce diverse forms. This is immediately plausible if religiosity is used as an illustration of content. That otherworldly desire can find its expression in the context of very different forms of religious leadership: in a strict sect with near dictatorial decision making, in a liberal parish with self-governing faithful, in a hierarchical church with bishops in charge, and so on. Similarly, the content of hunger resulting in economic interests has created in human history a wide variety of ordered interactions, like markets and business corporations, of which money is the form that interests Simmel (1907) most.

Every society creates within its domain equality on the one hand, so people can be replaced with each other, and on the other hand differentiation as inequality, so people can cooperate. And, as Durkheim (1893/1984) wrote, we can experience solidarity on the grounds of being similar: We are all unmarried males, or we are from the state of Texas. This acknowledgment of what we have in common has the potential to create a feeling of closeness. In a work environment, being similar can also mean that one of us can take over from the other and replace him or her because the required qualifications are the same. Surprisingly, Durkheim has pointed out, solidarity can also be based on the opposite condition, that of being different. If a person has abilities that I lack and vice versa, I can cooperate with my counterpart because then we can learn from each other and merge our special qualifications.

How Is Society Possible?

Simmel was influenced by the philosopher Kant and his idea that we humans create for ourselves an image of something, for instance "nature," and then make ourselves believe that we have actually observed it. What we see are trees, mountains, and sunrises, not "nature"; we may hear birds sing, but we do not hear "nature." Nobody has ever taken a photograph that captures "nature" as such. We all talk about nature because we share a concept of nature; however, it is not merely based on observations, but is largely the result of a collective mental construction. With this in mind, Kant asks the question, "How is nature possible?"

Inspired by Kant's reflections on nature, Simmel asked the analogous question, "How is society possible?" (Simmel, 1908a, 1908/2009). Here, too, nobody has ever presented a photograph or a video of "society." And yet, talk about society is widespread, not only among sociologists. To Kant, in his dealing with the question of how nature is possible, there are certain preconditions that must be met for the construction process to occur that leads to the notion of nature. Simmel asked what the preconditions are that make society possible. Following Kant's terminology, he referred to the preconditions as a priori principles (i.e., those principles that must be met before anything else can get underway).

The first of the principles is the fact that in describing what goes on in society, we cannot help but generalize. As a result, almost any statement about a person is skewed in the direction of generalization using familiar categories such as student, academic, mother, or politician. There are obviously vastly different types of students, but to make society possible they need to be generalized and, as it were, sorted into the catch-all box of the term *student*. That practice of generalization is a necessary consequence of the fact that complete knowledge of the individuality of others is not available to us. In order to make society possible, we form generalized impressions of our fellow humans and assign each of them to a general category despite the singularity of each individual. The impression is the image that one person gains of another person through interaction. As a result, we can attribute them to a particular sphere of interest and also decide whether or not a given person is a member of our own social circle.

The second a priori principle to make society possible is described by Simmel (1908/2009) like this: Every individual is "not only a part of society but also something else besides" (pp. 7, 45). If, for instance, a student works as a waiter to make extra money and is then called names by impatient customers, he can remind them as well as himself that he is something else besides being a waiter. In whatever way we are integrated into society by fulfilling certain prescribed tasks, according to Simmel, we must always hold back a part of personal existence from total identification with society.

This a priori principle takes into consideration the need to maintain a minimum level of mental health, for if infringed upon too much, there would be the risk of pathological developments both in the person and in social structure. Simmel saw the relationship between personal existence and identification with society as a dynamic process leading to a wide variety of different forms. In the context of those forms, "the a priori for empirical social life is that life is not entirely social." This means that how I appear in interactions with others depends on how I cultivate my independent, individual existence (Simmel, 1908/2009, p. 47).

Simmel's third a priori principle states the need of society for functional inequality. This is so because identical contributions to the common good will not lead to a division of labor: "Society is a construct of unlike parts. Since even where democratic or socialist tendencies anticipate or partially achieve an 'equality,' it is always a matter only of a similar evaluation of persons" (Simmel, 1908/2009, p. 49). There can be no question of the elements (and by that Simmel means the individuals who together form society) being homogeneous, in the sense of having identical qualities. In this diversity lies the prerequisite for cooperation. The assumption Simmel is leading up to here is that each individual can find a place in society because this ideally appropriate position for the individual in society does actually exist. It is the condition upon which the social life of the individual is based; it is why society is possible.

It has been the purpose of this chapter to explain that sociology's scholarly relatives are the humanities, not the natural sciences. That can be shown to result from the method by which the disparate data and facts found in research are molded into a unified picture of what there is to be known. The qualitative threshold that divides natural philosophy from social philosophy will become clear to anyone who, like Simmel, appreciates that when dealing with data relating to nature, unity is created merely in the mind of the researcher and that the objects of research remain unaffected by the researcher's mental activity. Society, in contrast, consists of conscious individuals, and their intellectual constructs create a unity (in circumstances that are the very object of investigation) not only within the individual but also as an immediate reality of society. Thus natural philosophy creates and studies processes that do not directly influence nature, whereas social philosophy must take account of processes of the conscious mind that themselves already are, and certainly influence, social reality.

Thus there is, for Simmel, a necessary transition from nature to society in which epistemology, as the branch of philosophy that studies the nature of knowledge, becomes empirical science. People are members, for instance, of the working class only to the extent to which they consider themselves members of the working class. Thus the nature of what goes on inside the person's head determines social reality, or at least codetermines it, and sociologists cannot ignore it. By 1908, the year he first published his *Soziologie*, Simmel's epistemology had reached a level that made it possible to adapt easily to a theory of society as the humanistic study of society.

Conclusion

Chapter 2 is devoted primarily to Simmel's method. He described the prevalence of the natural sciences over the humanities because the former promised progress and better living conditions. But he did not want to see the sciences become the sole source of orientation in life and the world. Because in the history of western civilization the split between arts and sciences could not be reconciled, Simmel placed sociology on the side of the humanities.

Sociology is needed because large social groups, like classes, take over from exceptional individuals the initiative in social change. It is sociology's primary task to develop new ways of looking at things and thus to apply an unfamiliar approach to familiar problems in the study of society. Society is possible provided three conditions are met: (a) individuals are generalized into categories of people; (b) a person's integration into society always leaves out some personal aspects due to his or her uniqueness; and (c) the collectivity demands that all members are different so they can find their special place in society compatible with their unique individuality.

This second chapter has maybe helped open the debate about these issues:

- Why does Simmel not want the natural sciences to become the sole source of orientation in culture and society?
- Why does Simmel see sociology on the side of the humanities rather than the sciences?
- How can sociology be acknowledged as an independent discipline if it does not claim a list of topics reserved for its own research and teaching?
- Simmel spells out the conditions under which society is possible. But what if society is not possible?

3

Individualization as Ethical Concern

The Stranger and the Courage to Be Different

In the context of designing a novel discipline of scholarship, Simmel points out that sociology finds its justification, in part, from the fact that history is no longer seen as merely the result of individual intentions and decisions of a few greats but as the result of **social movements** that are actions of the masses and classes. This means a shift from the individual to the collective in method. However, his ethical concern points in the opposite direction. He wants to interpret social development as the gradual evolution and refinement of the individual, and as a result, he is optimistic about future social movements being geared toward an increase in personal freedom.

Simmel had great respect for the innate potential of individuals. He hoped that more personal freedom would mean the realization of more positive individual gifts. This optimism had the following foundation: Simmel believed that humans have the ability and the duty to develop their talents. In his writings on religion there is a moving illustration for that notion, when Simmel recounts one of Martin Buber's Hasidic tales: the story of a Rabbi by the name of Meir who speculates with his students what will happen to them when they die and face God upon their arrival in the beyond.

The rabbi first assumes that God may ask him, "Meir, why did you not become Moses?" The answer to that will simply be "Because I am only Meir." This would then reflect humility as well as the rejection of an alien pattern of personal development. The same would apply to a second hypo-thetical question by God: "Why did you not become Ben Akiba?" Answer: "Because I am only Meir." But in the end, the rabbi imagines that God may ask him, "Meir, why did you not become Meir?" This leads to the religious man's desperate question directed toward his assembled students: "What shall my answer be then?" Because having missed one's calling by not becoming what one is destined to be would be a frightening admission of failure (Simmel, 1997, p. xiv).

However, developing one's unique abilities in order to become what one is destined to be—attractive as that may sound—often requires the courage to endure isolation. Peer group pressure usually levels individual abilities down to the group average. Students with exceptional interests, like art or archeology, frequently find no sympathy among classmates. Following one's calling, then, seems to demand sacrifice in popularity and may even lead to the individual finding himself or herself in the position of an outsider, similar to a stranger. As we shall see, Simmel was fully aware of this problem. He viewed the stranger in the history of culture as a courageous outsider.

One of the most widely read and quoted texts by Simmel is his "Excursus on the Stranger" (Simmel, 1908b, 1908/2009). It contains his reflections on the interplay between society, with its demands for conformity, and the indi-viduals with the strength to be different. Simmel invites us to imagine two social groups, which he gives the meaningless names M and N. At the outset, they are sharply distinct from one another, in terms of their typical charac-teristics and their respective attitudes and beliefs.

This is, however, only the point of departure for a dynamic view of what happens to the groups after they contact each other. Each consists of homo-geneous (very similar) and closely related members. Next, before the impact of the other group is felt, in Simmel's model for change the increase in mem-bership of the group gives rise to more and more differentiation within it: The more there are, the more they try to be somehow special in order to achieve recognition.

As a consequence, what were originally minimal differences among indi-viduals, in terms of outward and inner disposition and its expression, become increasingly noticeable due to the necessity of surviving in the face of fiercer competition, with increasingly unconventional means of specializa-tion for emphasizing individual uniqueness. No matter how varied the points of departure of the groups M and N may have been, the two will gradually resemble each other more and more because only a relatively lim-ited number of essential human "formations" is available, and their number can only increase gradually (Simmel, 1908b, p. 710). (The limited number of available alternatives can be observed, for instance, in the context of reforms in institutions of higher learning: Frequently after two or three generations of reformers, the "innovation" is back to the same conditions where the predecessors of the current leaders started making changes).

There are numerous reports in the literature of cultural anthropology of the effects of strangeness on social evolution (Bargatzky, 1978). The **stranger** who represents an unknown culture and country is usually welcomed and even protected under strict rules of hospitality. In most cases, the members of the indigenous culture know, or at least sense, their chance to learn something new from their visitor. Also, he or she is most likely welcome if he or she arrives alone or with very few companions: One stranger is seen as a courageous and creative individualist and likely greeted as potential innovator; a whole group of strangers, on the other hand, may be experienced as a threat and as a gang of invaders or spies and treated accordingly (Haag, 2011, p. 53f.).

What is peculiar about Simmel's approach to these phenomena is his relational view of the effects of *strangeness*. A person is not strange, but the relationship that is established with him or her is marked by the imposition of strangeness. It is, in other words, socially defined as strange. The stranger comes from far away and has the potential to leave again because he cannot be forced to stay. This sets him or her aside from the normal local people, who usually do not have the option to leave. Because of the special condition under which strangers participate in the daily interactions, they are treated differently. Thus the relationship that is established with them is a strange relationship, and those participating in it experience strangeness as a result of the interpretation that they themselves ascribe to it.

The presence of the often foreign or—increasingly in contemporary terminology—alien person reminds the members of the host society that they ought to consider changing their ways. The effect is the experience of ambivalence: On the one hand, they welcome new ideas, but at the same time, they often see critique of their status quo as an unwelcome provocation, and they may take their anger out on the newcomer. This brings us back to the two groups that Simmel calls "M" and "N." They start out being different but end up appearing similar.

At the same time, although the groups become more standard, the person becomes more and more unique; he or she is less and less a uniform product of his or her social environment. Thus, according to Simmel, eventually individualization not only profits the person who makes use of his or her talents, but it initiates global social change and reduces the differences between nations, provided there are enough courageous men or women who have the strength to be different.

In his analysis of rational capitalism, Max Weber describes the tension between two ethical impacts within the context of Christianity. This is relevant to the impact of strangeness on change. Weber points out that the reversal of Christianity from **universalism** to **exclusivity** was crucial for developing utterly successful business ethics oriented toward gainful investment: Pre-reformation churches emphasized the brotherhood of all men (universalism), while Calvinist Protestantism spread among the baptized the notion of being a member of the chosen few, similar to the self-confidence of the Jewish people (exclusivity). The former rewarded conformity; the latter encouraged being different and having the courage to become a stranger.

Societies that were consistently universalist had no ethical foundation for making any difference between persons: They all were children of God, regardless whether they acknowledged that or not (Simmel, 1997, p. 203). If one of them turned out to be poor or in distress it was the brotherly duty of his fellow Christian to come to his or her aid. Granted, this did not always happen in real life, but it was nevertheless a referent to ethics with powerful implications for a strong drive toward equality as an ethical and political goal: Do unto thy neighbors as you would have them do unto you!

But who is that neighbor of mine? He is not the member of my own ethnic group or clan; he is the stranger from a despised population nearby, like the inhabitants of Samaria! Here Simmel may have seen a point of departure for his stranger. It is he, the stranger, who brings about progress, healing, and help from afar. The person with the strength to be different initiates the change that is needed to make equal opportunity for all more likely! This is the fascination emanating from the ambivalence between universalism and exclusivity.

The specific, rational type of capitalism Max Weber set out to study did not originate in the traditional universalistic cultures of Catholic and Orthodox Christianity in Italy, Spain, Russia, and Greece, in part maybe because everybody was everybody else's brother in Christ and had no right to witness his or her poverty unmoved. What was needed to justify the wealth of some compared to the poverty of others was an *exclusive* ethics, as was frequently deduced from a sacred text: "You are not allowed to take interest from your brother. From the stranger you may take interest" (Deuteronomy 23:20). In this religious passage, the stranger is not the clansman, but he is a partner in a business transaction (Nelson, 1969). As is well known, Muslims also are not allowed to take interest. Against this background it is plausible that modern capitalism did not develop well in areas where the religion of Islam is prevalent.

Be that as it may, it appears that there are two distinct sets of values that can be functional in overcoming sentimental feelings of compassion, so inappropriate in commercial dealings and certainly an impediment for the development of rational capitalism: One is the Protestant ethic as described by

Max Weber (1904/1920), the other is Benjamin Nelson's (1969) concept of tribalism. They can be sketched as follows:

1. Calvinist teaching on predestination made a Protestant ethic possible, according to which God, in his unfathomable grace, has chosen a few to be his children, to be saved, and to become successful and wealthy, whereas those poor "devils" who remained needy were simply not chosen by God. Who am I to worry about them, if even the Almighty has decided against them? This conviction gives the individual the courage to stand against the imposition of conformity and to be different from the rest of them. Indeed, typically, social and economic change was initiated by minorities who felt strong enough to be strangers and to resist the pressure of being like everybody else.

2. Contrary to the ancient version of Christian ethics, according to which a minority of "strangers" confronts the vast majority of universalist conformers, under the condition of tribalism the innovative persons are all members of small minorities: their respective clans. They thus find themselves surrounded by others with the same background. This may become the prevalent condition in the foreseeable future when progressive individualization will lead to people increasingly experiencing each other as being equally peculiar. The "stranger" is then functioning in the market as a normal and daily phenomenon. He does that in negotiations on the side of supply as well as on that of demand. The market, accordingly, is a forum of interaction where clansmanship on the one end and strangeness on the other end of the social spectrum collaborate in a very successful fashion, at least in the economy.

Toward an Ethics of Individualization

Simmel presents his own concept of ethics that is neither tribal nor national, nor even general; his concept is personal. He rejects a vague submission of the individual to the current unspecific general rules in the writings of Kant; instead, he encourages the question of what individuals owe to themselves, as was illustrated by the discourse between Rabbi Meir and his students. It is along this same line of reasoning, namely that each person must follow his or her unique calling, that Simmel criticizes Kant. As we saw in Chapter 1, Kant proposed the ethical principle that our conduct ought to be guided by rules that can be generalized for all human beings (a principle commonly referred to as *categorical imperative*). Simmel rejects that because it values conformity over uniqueness.

By contrast, he asks, "Can I not demand more of myself than of my average fellow citizen? Can I therefore not impose more stringent rules upon myself than upon others?" So while Kant's egalitarian ethics is designed to prevent people from finding an easy way out for themselves, it also prevents them from performing anything above average. Simmel criticizes Kant's categorical imperative for not taking into account the heroic and exceptionally good person. Kant may have had in mind an approach in ethics that would insure equality, but, according to Simmel, at the same time Kant also cut off the chance for a unique individual to overperform and to establish his or her level of ethical orientation above the broad average of everybody else as a stranger.

Accordingly, the thought of **individualization** emerges here as an evolutionary tendency that is inherent in the mutual exchange among persons. The emphasis on the growing respect for personal uniqueness will—according to Simmel—increase the tolerance within groups and permit individuals to be different from a general uniform standard. That, in turn, will encourage people to go beyond original boundaries imposed on group members in terms of spatial, economic, and mental relationships. In addition, the tolerance within groups serves as a push to place next to the initial "centripetalism of the individual group, a centrifugal tendency as a bridge to other groups, with growing individualization" of its members (Simmel, 1908/2009, p. 623).

For Simmel, the quality of uniqueness called *individuality* may either be derived from characteristics of the individual or from those of the group to which he or she belongs. The egalitarian and conformist model works on the basis of a contract between group and person like this: The group can demand conformity to its standards, and in return for following them, the individual is endowed with a kind of individuality based on belonging to that particular group.

In his example of the Quakers, Simmel shows how the close religious connection among the faithful combined with an emphasis on uniformity in behavior and attire tends toward anchoring individuality in the community rather than in the person (Simmel, 1890a, p. 49; Helle, 2013, p. 49). In the course of social evolution, the prevalent source of identity has shifted gradually from the group to the individual person. This makes it easier to find a place for an odd person to fit in, but at the same time, it makes it harder to find a replacement for a human being who is lost due to death or desertion.

In this context, Simmel looks at the way people deal with fashion and changing fads in society and interprets that against the background of the inability to cultivate a personal uniqueness out of fear of responsibility. The frustration resulting from the tacit admission that each individual has the duty to cultivate his or her potential, together with the awareness of failure on this front, often leads a person to produce external uniqueness by wearing fashionable things and striking hairdos. This may be accompanied by a fear of isolation that may lead to bitterness and peculiarity rather than be experienced as a chance for individualization under the conditions of modernity.

Simmel points to the importance of the family in preventing the negative effects of modernization. Chapter 5 will be devoted to Simmel's sociology of the family. The narrow circle of close relatives in kinship groups is seen by him as an opportunity to balance the demands for rationality and emotional detachment in public. The high esteem in which Simmel holds the family as an intermediate social form in the context of his theory of social evolution is remarkable. Family ties are needed to fend off isolation, which if excessive—Simmel assumes—will lead to psychic deformation (Helle, 2013, p. 50).

The evolution of culture and society is tied to the coordination of processes on these separate levels: (a) the individual, (b) the family, (c) the group of friends and neighbors as intermediate between family and society, (d) society itself or a person's country, and finally (e) global humankind. Simmel shares the optimistic faith in a movement toward a world society in which first the intellectuals and later all those who are cosmopolitan in orientation feel interconnected with each other.

The history of the global dream of worldwide companionship goes back to aspects of ancient Christian faith and was revived in the Romantic period, as exemplified by the lyrics to the concluding movement of Beethoven's Ninth Symphony. This dream turns up again in the demand by Karl Marx for all proletarians of all countries to unite. Marxist hopes for a world society were then shattered in the German version of a National Socialism during Hitler and with more lasting consequences in the proclamation of a special Chinese type of socialism.

His ideas of the innate dynamics of society led Simmel to his project of evolutionary ethics: One of his basic values is **equality**, but he distinguishes sharply between different concepts of equality. The attempt to make persons equal by putting them in uniforms is totally unacceptable to him. Uniformity cannot result in a human form of equality. Rather, an equality that is ethically based can only be realized by acknowledging that the incomparable individuality of each person is something exceedingly valuable. When this incomparability and uniqueness of the individual is accepted as an undisputed property of all, only then is the type of equality generated that Simmel accepts because it interconnects each one as a person in a society rather than as a number within the anonymous masses.

Simmel thus advocates a concept according to which equality is achieved through the acknowledgment and realization of everyone's claim to uniqueness and individuality. Following equality, the value of unity is introduced to prevent social evolution from leading to isolation and loneliness. Simmel's idea of unity leads him to a position according to which mutual exchange—understood as an interaction in which one person helps the other move toward self-realization—creates and solidifies unity step by step. His emphasis on individual uniqueness is compatible with the project of a worldwide community: Sooner or later we will all be strangers respecting each other's uniqueness.

Simmel has been called the expert on modernity by David Frisby (1944–2010) and others. The scholarly discourse on modernity, in turn, has led to the distinction between different types of modernity (Eisenstadt, 2000; Beck & Grande, 2010). Modernity, whatever that may be, was for Simmel not a state of affairs but a process. Simmel was an early champion of **processual thinking**, and we will have to look in more detail at what that means.

Process Plus Stability

In Greece, as early as 500 years before our common era, the necessity of a dynamic concept of reality was recognized by Heraclitus of Ephesus (535–475 BC) and his students. Therefore the theory of change is rooted not in Darwin but in Heraclitus and his school. According to Plato, Socrates said in the course of his oral teaching, to which his student Plato listened, "It was Heraclitus who said, Everything flows on; nothing stays in place." Heraclitus is also quoted as having said, "You cannot step twice into the same river," meaning that the river has changed between the two times because it flows on (Graham, 2011). Yet, it is, of course, still the same river. How else could we describe that it has changed?

The very notion of change presupposes that there is something that remains identical to itself, for otherwise we could not even talk about development as referring to a person or a thing that is still the same, even though somewhat different. Socrates is supposed to have given a speech on love that dealt with this problem: Even in the life of the same individual there is succession and not absolute unity.

> A man is called the same, and yet in the short interval which elapses between youth and age . . . he is undergoing a perpetual process of loss and reparation—hair, flesh, bones, blood, and the whole body are always changing.

Which is true not only of the body, but also of the soul, whose habits, tempers, opinions, desires, pleasures, pains, fears, never remain the same in any one of us. (Kraut, 2012)

But he or she remains the same person. And indeed, Heraclitus also developed his processual thinking against a stable background: "The only political attitude which we can safely extrapolate from the fragments is a lucid, almost Hobbesian appreciation of the fact that civilized life and communal survival depend upon loyalty to the law" (Graham, 2011). So we have here in Heraclitus himself the two aspects of a particular style of thought: awareness of the fluidity of reality, as the changing river, and maintenance of the identity of what is developing, in the case of Heraclitus as loyalty to the law.

This same duality of thought, process plus stability, can be discerned in Simmel's social thought. Let us start with stability: Simmel pursues as a theme that runs through his publications the topic of personal identity. In traditional society, a person became an adult sometime between the ages of 18 and 21. Having grown to that age typically meant that the person was mature and well-developed and was not expected to change too much after that, except of course by getting old. Spouses, who married at that age because they loved each other and fit well as companions, could rely on still being a match years later. In modern society, in a happy case, they may continue to develop their personalities and develop and learn further in tandem and in a parallel way, so that ideally they change together and in the same direction. However, frequently one of the spouses develops one way and the other a different way (or not at all), and suddenly they may realize that they have grown apart.

This creates the potential for fear. If I go out to study, to travel, to work in remote and alien environments, if I have all these new and exciting experiences, will the persons close to me still recognize me and accept me after I return? This is the question of identity: Will I still be recognized as being identical to myself? Will the people who know me say, "He (or she) has changed!" or will they say, "He (or she) has become a different person."? The second case may be described as a loss of identity: The returning person, for better or for worse, is no longer experienced as identical with the person who went out to learn new things.

Simmel, during the very first decade as author of scholarly publications, drew attention to his social thought with a two-volume book on ethics (Simmel, 1892, 1893). There he beseeches his readers to follow him in looking for philosophical foundations for a dynamic approach to ethics. Traditional ethics had been bogged down with the dictum by Plato that anything that claims to be true must be unchanging. The background, tied more or less to common human weaknesses, is this: If I accept some statement as being the truth, I would like to assume that two years from now the same statement will still be true, if I use the same wording. Although this is totally plausible, Simmel presents it as highly problematic if applied to ethics because culture and society evolve over time. His reasoning is as follows.

The conditions under which humans lived in 2010 were, in many parts of the world, so vastly different from those of 1810 that it is flatly unreasonable to ask them to follow the same rules. For example, it is obvious that many rules, like speed limits on highways, could not possibly exist in the absence of automobiles. So, the case for a dynamic approach to ethics can be made easily in the area of technology, traffic, and others. But there are much more sensitive areas, like the way we conduct our private lives, where the general public tend to cling to the old rules for fear that any new rules may result in chaos. This is also understandable with regard to the widespread anxiety that total loss of orientation will prevail, for instance in people's marital and sexual lives.

To argue against these fears, Simmel refers to the topic of identity. We normally have an innate urge to remain who we are. If I return to acquaintances whom I have not seen for a long time, I of course hope that they will still recognize me and acknowledge me as the person they knew some time ago. This urge, the hope to retain my identity even though I may undergo considerable change, is the point of departure for Simmel's ethics. He teaches that what I decide to do today must be congruent with my personal way of developing. The deeds I perform now should not make me blush when I look in the mirror tomorrow.

By tying my behavior to the continuity inherent in my personal identity, I am not turned loose; I am not a freewheeling agent of spontaneity, even though I may no longer simply follow traditional rules in every situation of my life. I am not out of control because I am subject to the inner rules of my own identity, and those may be quite strict, indeed. But the result may, of course, be that what is good for me (and those close to me) may not be good for everybody. I am allowed to think that everything changes and everyone is different. So I will insist on doing what I think is right even though others do not understand me. The established system of ethics should not treat everybody the same, and we should adopt a new dynamic ethics. This is what Simmel suggests. As one can easily imagine, his point of view was not generally popular a century ago, nor can it be expected to be popular today.

Admittedly, there is immediate danger on the horizon: How to allow for the obvious fact that there are selfish and irresponsible people out there? In our Latin class we may have learned the idiom *quod licet Jovi non licet bovi*, meaning what is allowed for Jupiter is not allowed to the cattle in the field.

But Simmel is surprisingly optimistic, knowing that his readers and listeners are educated people, and he expects them not to take advantage of their privileged position in society but interpret their status as an above-average level of responsibility. Consequently, I must be able to do special things that cannot be recommended for everybody to do. And in addition, responsibility means that I am not free to do anything I want in a particular moment without thinking much about the consequences. What I do now must allow me still to be able to say yes to it in the future. I do not need to be ashamed of what I did because it is justified by the continuity of my personal life and by the unique situation I was in when I did it.

The history of culture repeatedly refers to "teachers" who did not count among those with whom they grew up because those learned men did not follow traditional ethical rules. Being a "prophet" has frequently been a life-threatening profession. Unfortunately this fate was not limited to religious personages. Socrates was ordered to drink poison because he was perceived to be misguiding the youth of Athens. Plato witnessed the trial of Socrates but was too ill to be present at the death of his beloved teacher. Being known as a follower of Socrates, Plato felt threatened in Athens. Disillusioned with the corruption and petty politics in Athens, Plato immigrated to southern Italy.

There Plato served a tyrant as court philosopher until the ruler came to dislike the sage's ideas. Accordingly, the tyrant sold Plato into slavery for a good price. Had not a good friend purchased him and set him free, he would have remained a slave for the rest of his life. Later, back in Athens, Aristotle started an academy only to find himself subject to accusations similar to those that had led to the death of Socrates. As a result, Aristotle had to flee his native Athens to save his life. This is a sobering review of some of the early innovators, and of course—alas—the list of these strangers is far from complete. Fortunately, the people of Athens today identify with the victims, not the perpetrators of the old days.

Simmel presupposes that problems arising from the dynamization of ethics can be made a topic of empirical study. However, such research should itself not be burdened down with preconceived ethical concepts: "Just as the pathologist is not expected to pass judgment on the aesthetic value of a corpse being dissected by him, so the person involved in research about ethics should not moralize about the morals he studies" (Simmel, 1893, p. v). This is an early statement about the principle of value-free research in the social sciences.

Anticipating the potential results of such research, Simmel explains why the need for an evolutionary ethics will grow. Orienting life toward firmly founded values and following ideals guaranteeing unquestioned goals in life will become more and more difficult (Simmel, 1893, p. 18). This will be the effect of weakening religious conviction and of critical thinking, which together make it less and less likely that traditional ideals of political, religious, or personal origin are being followed with unquestioned devotion. However, the fact that such orientations will be more difficult to entertain does not mean that the need for them has also disappeared. This observation points to a growing gap between supply and demand in the "market" for ethics and religion.

The evolution of society from a stage in which merely the narrow circles of kinship, tribalism, and community are relevant to stages in which wider and wider social circles become available, eventually leading to a worldwide field of interaction, must necessarily lead to an evolution of ethics. In fact, these two strains of development, the opening up of social structure and the dynamization of morals, depend on each other. The result of this reflection is the insight that even in identical situations, different people will act differently without thereby necessarily contradicting any general principle of moral behavior.

This effect of individualization frequently alienates the person from his or her primary associations, but at the same time, it makes it easier to be in contact with a large number of persons of different orientations. Provided the dynamization of ethics can keep up with this structural evolution, Simmel (1892, 1893) sees the chance for breaking down barriers between the respective morals of social classes, nations, and other groupings and replacing them with a global ethics of respect for the uniqueness of the individual as a fellow human being (1893, p. 30).

Conclusion

Chapter 3 deals with the structure of society and with prescriptions for how people should conduct themselves. The latter are usually referred to as "social norms." Simmel sees change on both levels of analysis: The structure opens up, allowing us to live in wider company; the norms require making adjustments to this evolution by devising ideas for a dynamic ethics. These changes are the requirements to be met in order to enable individualization to progress as the decisive trait of modernization. To Simmel, a central task for the modern person is to recognize and develop to the fullest his or her innate potential. Fulfillment of this task hinges on the courage of the individual to be different to the point of becoming a stranger.

Systems of ethics can be distinguished by either emphasizing brotherly closeness among all humans (universalism) or stressing the superiority of a certain group of people (exclusivity). Although universalism as a program may result in changes that make the world more peaceful, as an established condition it lacks tolerance for strangeness and leads to stable, but potentially rigid, conditions. Exclusivity, on the other hand, encourages strangeness and accordingly promotes change. Individuals may be reluctant to live the lives of innovators for two reasons: (a) fear of losing the approval of friends and other persons close to them and (b) fear of loss of identity. Many of the great innovators had to endure persecution and exile. They are remembered today for their courage as well as their contribution to evolution.

- Simmel promotes a dynamic approach to ethics. But how can that be implemented without causing confusion and insecurity among people who want to know what they ought to do?
- If more and more persons feel encouraged to live their lives as strangers, then how can anyone find orientation and rules for developing his or her own personality?
- How can universalistic and exclusive principles of ethics be reconciled in a society without breakdown of consensus and undue factionalism?
- How does one draw the line between courageous insistence on individualistic self-fulfillment on the one hand and loving consideration for relatives and friends on the other?

4

What Religions Have in Common

Life After Death

Simmel's approach to religion can be described as closely related to a pragmatist concept of "truth." To Simmel, the truth is not only what works but, more important, the basis on which the believer is prepared to work or, more generally, is prepared to act. In times of deep disappointments and hopelessness, people are inclined to only rely on what they can put their hands on. That attitude of distrust is expected to save the skeptic from becoming the victim of all kinds of false prophets. Catastrophic events like wars, plagues, and famines tend to have radical effects on religions: They make some people give up their faith and cause others to emerge from the tribulations with an even stronger religious orientation. As we will see, Simmel argues that *religions* may lose their credibility, but the individual's need for *religiousness* is there to stay, regardless of what happens to religions.

What all religions have in common is the conviction that death does not end the existence of the person and that the living may experience some personal attention from the beyond. Of course, how this is written into concrete creeds varies greatly from religion to religion, but no religion will teach that there is no life after death. Also, all religions will expect the living to get into contact with a person in the beyond by prayer, sacrifice, meditation, or other ritual. The "person" may be a god, a saint, a deceased ancestor, or a benign or evil spirit. Thus, to the sociologist of religion, who is interested—as a sociologist should be—in what goes on *between* persons, the religious person can be identified as being in a relationship with an immortal and feeling thus guided, assisted, or threatened from a person in the beyond.

No religious person will believe in anything unless he or she is convinced that it really exists. Humans of all ages seem to have given their religious ideas the status of reality. In the process of doing that, they can only imagine *problems of life and death* in terms of their *experience of life and death*. Those experiences were needed to provide convincing images for the content of faith. Research about religion includes shedding some light on the conditions under which people give certain content of their consciousness the status of reality and thus call it their "unquestionable faith." This entails the likelihood that the imagination of the sacred will be mistaken for the sacred itself. It also explains, in part, why in the Jewish religion, in Evangelical Christianity, in Islam, and in early Daoism the faithful are not allowed to make an image of God lest the image become an idol.

Similar to Simmel's distinction between the content as religiosity of the individual and the form it is given as religion in a given society, William James writes about the feelings people have toward the sacred versus the expression this finds in religious philosophy. The former, feelings toward the sacred, supplies the content, which then needs to be given a specific form in order to find expression in a given society. Interestingly, James does not confront emotions and reason as conflicting alternatives, but instead sees reason as an aid in giving form to religiosity: "To redeem religion from unwholesome privacy, and to give public status and universal right of way to its deliverances, has been reason's task" (James, 1901/1902, p. 284).

Simmel agrees with **pragmatism** that a person considers those ideas upon which he or she will act to be real. Truth and reality are the crucial qualities attributed to contents of faith. Traditional religious dogma that cannot maintain these characteristics will sink down in collective consciousness to the level of fairytales and King Arthur–type lore. The difference between religions and other worldviews is, in addition to the requirements of truth and reality, that religions must be able to establish a living relationship between the believer and an immortal. Unless a personal relationship with some well-known counterpart in the beyond can be established, religion has no chance of acceptance.

The divine person may be a god, a saint, an ancestor, or a spirit of some kind. The common denominator of all these alternatives is a combination of (a) immortality and (b) effectiveness. In other words, the believer must be able to address someone who, for him or her, (a) is real (i.e., truly exists out there), (b) is eternal (i.e., will not suddenly disappear due to death or desertion), and (c) is powerful (i.e., he or she can do something for or against me).

Other worldviews that Simmel would not count among the religions (without thereby making a value judgment of whether they are more or less desirable) suggest faith in impersonal energies that reside in nature or space. They may be powerful, but they cannot be engaged in dialogue because they lack the quality of persons. Faith in a New Age or some iron law in history, for instance, can deeply impact the convictions and actions of people, but it would not be meaningful, in the context of Simmel's approach, to describe belief systems of this type as religions, although, of course, as convictions with other characteristics they deserve everybody's respect.

The dividing line may be very thin: If I worship my ancestors, believing that they can influence my life, help me, and be helped by me, for instance by offering a sacrifice for them, then that condition would qualify as religious. If, on the other hand, my ancestors are simply commemorated in ritual ways without the expectation that they can have an impact on the lives of the living, then that may be an aspect of a religion, but it is itself not a religion because the addressees of the belief are not experienced as having power. Accordingly, if a Christian deposits flowers at the grave of his beloved dead grandparent, that obviously is not ancestor worship.

If all religions share the property of establishing personal contact with one or more immortals, then the sociology of religion ought to establish a typology of the variety of those transcendental contacts. Some immortals are—at least for some mortals—well-known because they lived on this earth at one time. That applies to Christian saints (to some extent, provided their story is still told) and to Chinese ancestors (to a more likely extent, provided their descendants can remember them). In those cases when the human ability of thinking and remembering is not sufficient to reveal the existence of objective truth, it is necessary—and therefore also legitimate—to *define* such truth as given. What today every sociologist knows as the "definition of the situation" owes its foundations to Simmel's theory of knowledge. It arrived, most likely in Chicago, by the intercession of Robert E. Park who, as I mentioned at the end of Chapter 1, was Simmel's student in Berlin.

A Way of Looking at the World

In the history of culture, the definition of what is to be counted as real can largely be studied as the achievement—for better or for worse—of religious belief systems. The study of religious definitions of reality is, then, the primary task of a history-oriented sociology of religion. But what did this branch of sociology achieve so far? Anyone whose interest has led her to look for early literature in that branch will think about Max Weber's

(1904/1920) journal article "The Protestant Ethic and the Spirit of Capitalism." Other "classics" in sociology also have contributed significantly to the study of religion. Perhaps the best known of them is Émile Durkheim. In his book *The Elementary Forms of Religious Life* (1912), he presented a pragmatist and functionalist approach to religion.

Weber and Durkheim could both build on what August Comte (1842) wrote about religious consciousness. The "theological stage"—religious consciousness—is the first of the three stages in which Comte believed human thought to have developed. As is well known, Karl Marx (1844/1985) referred to religion as a leftover from the times of superstition and a political sign of a lack of emancipation—as the "opium of the people." Many students of sociology will mention Comte, Marx, Durkheim, and Weber as important authors who made religion the subject of their research and publications. But only very few are familiar with Georg Simmel as a sociologist of religion.

What was Simmel's point of departure for his interest in religion as a topic of scholarly activity? Faced with the effects of early industrialism, he expected a cultural crisis resulting from the increasing contradictions between the subjective and the objective. What had been objectified as literature and art, as custom and tradition, became more and more foreign to the person living with it. The worst example for the process Simmel had in mind is described by Max Weber as the unending trend toward bureaucratization from which we are suffering to this day.

But there was and is hope in culture—in art and religion as well as in scholarship—and Simmel turns to the study of these phenomena, and particularly to the sociology of religion, for relief. During the last two decades of his life, from 1898 to 1918, he devoted much of his writing to religion. The scholarly study of religion has been faced with the empirical problem of antagonism between different religions and with the theoretical problem of a bias toward the Judeo-Christian traditions of the West to the disadvantage of Asian religions. Simmel contributed to remedying that defect.

What is the method with which Simmel approached the problems of religion?

1. To him, religion is not a clearly delineated province of reality, like the political organization of the state or the economy; rather, it is a way of looking at the world, like an attitude or a perspective. Simmel does not reduce religion to fleeting emotions that may or may not occur within the individual; to him, religion, like art, is a "third realm" between the subject and the object with the potential of mediating and mitigating the conflict between them.

2. Religion thus contributes to the construction of that bridge between the person and the world that surrounds him or her. It "is always an objectification of the subject and therefore has its place beyond that reality which is attached to the object as such or to the subject as such" (Simmel, 1919, p. 29).

3. A third component of Simmel's method is the dialectic of form and content. We have dealt with that here before in another context in Chapter 2. Simmel points out that the idea of God as *content* may be expressed in the *form* of either pious meditation or intellectual reflection. Only in the first case would Simmel consider the result a religious phenomenon. If the second applied, however, the form of rational analysis probably would bar it from leading to religiosity. The content, thinking about God, may be derived from religion, but the form it is given deprives it of the quality of religiousness. In order to clarify that distinction even further, Simmel—in his texts from 1902 on—makes the distinction between *religion* and *religiosity*. According to this somewhat surprising approach, much of what goes on as scholarly reflection in theology would *not* qualify as being religious in *form*.

Simmel (1997, pp. 121–133) further illustrates his position in his 1902 essay "Contributions to the Epistemology of Religion" with the prayer for faith. From the perspective of rational argumentation, it is pointless to pray for faith because such a prayer would only make sense if the existence of a deity that can be addressed in the prayer is already assumed as given. Then a prayer for faith would be redundant. The prayer would be asking for confirmation of a reality that, by the fact that praying occurs, is already assumed as given. Simmel, however, defines faith as the individual's ability to give to religious *content* a *form* derived from personal *religiosity* instead of having been derived from intellectual reflection. To pray for faith is then entirely plausible, either because the individual may feel the need for the deity to intervene on that issue or because the very practice of praying may produce the desired effect: making the *form* of a pious frame of mind become habitual.

4. A fourth tool Simmel uses in the study of religion is another pair of terms: *center* and *periphery*. Humans are free to the extent that the center of their being determines its periphery because the reverse is not possible. What is unique and utterly personal would fill the center; that which many people have in common can be only peripheral to individuals because that will not help them confirm their identity from inside themselves. (Simmel, 1997, p. 195f). Simmel critically observes that Christian churches have tended to concentrate on peripheral qualities that all believers have in common, rather than encouraging each soul to use its unique talents (see Matthew 25: 26–27).

Simmel is convinced that neither he nor anybody else can make any learned statement about what may or may not exist in the beyond. It is simply not the business of philosophy or sociology to try to do that. The eternal truths are beyond the scope of scholarship; they cannot be known empirically. Simmel's approach saves students of religion the embarrassment of either assuming without proof that there is something in the beyond or, by contrast, that there is nothing. The factual existence or nonexistence of sacred persons and objects is neither assumed nor denied; it is plainly left undecided, and thus gives Simmel's method the ideological neutrality that is needed in scholarship.

At the same time, the changing images of the sacred—whether they are simply figments of the imagination or more or less successful attempts at reconstructing an incomprehensible eternal reality—can and must be studied empirically: They are empirically present in this world in the minds of living persons as content that potentially relates the individual to the beyond. What is open and accessible to scholarly research are thus the bridges that humans build in association with each other to come as close as they can to experiencing and understanding the eternal truths and the immortal persons that stand for them, provided those truths and immortal persons do exist.

Therefore, Simmel's writings on religion contain no confrontation between objective transcendental facts that a certain religious community may confess as its creed and the subjective impressions that may become the perspective of a pious mind. The two are independent realities. Religion, as co-created and objectified by interacting believers, has become a *third realm,* like art and scholarship, with the potential to mediate between what may (or may not) actually exist in the beyond and the person puzzled by the question of what he or she ought to believe in.

Simmel combines his heuristic tools with the hypothesis of an evolution of religious ideas throughout human history. The notion of evolution neither deprives man of the dignity of creative freedom nor does it preclude any divine intervention. It is but a heuristic tool to help organize and categorize human concepts about God and the sacred. In order to test how fruitful the method may be, it must be applied also to Asian religions, not only to Judaism and Christianity. In their comparative studies, sociologists of religion can only try to *describe* the religious ideas people have, including what is true and real *to them.* The confrontation between what is believed to be eternally unchanging and what obviously evolves over time is, of course, seen and discussed by Simmel.

In 1909, Simmel (1997, pp. 3–6) published his text "Fundamental Religious Ideas and Modern Science: An Inquiry." In it we can observe him apply the methodological tools that have been enumerated here above. He points to the difficulties that religion confronts due to the conflict between "religiousness as an inner state or need of man and all the traditional lore which, as the content of that inner state, is offered as a means to fulfill these needs" (p. 3). Frequently the advance of science has been introduced as a reason for the loss of religious conviction. Religion is then seen as a stopgap needed only until research into the order of nature has advanced far enough to prove that miracles make no sense.

Simmel (1997) rejects this notion as erroneous:

> A child born of a virgin, water being transformed into wine, a deceased man ascending to heaven: None of this has become less probable as a result of 19th-century science than it was according to the experience of people living in the 13th century. (p. 3)

Therefore, what makes it increasingly difficult to accept traditional faith has nothing, or very little, to do with the insights arrived at by the advances of modern natural sciences. There must be other reasons. Those can be found, according to Simmel, not so much in what the sciences came up with as the *results* of their research, but rather in the *methods* they used in conducting it. The test of truth has shifted from the testimony of reliable witnesses to what I myself can investigate and prove by way of laboratory research.

It is not the statements about empirical reality promulgated and backed by science that weaken religion; rather, it is "the spirit of science as a whole, by the application of basic scientific attitudes to what is not investigable, and by the tendency to define as believable reality only that which is scientifically probable" (Simmel, 1997, p. 4). So, *it is indeed* the advancement of science that causes the problem for religion, but not in the way that is generally assumed to be the case: The criterion for *what is real* has changed, and as a consequence the quality of truth has become attributed to personal and individual experience in a laboratory. And this is increasingly the case because, as was mentioned at the beginning of this chapter, in times of deep disappointments and hopelessness, people are inclined to only rely on what they can put their hands on. But why should that be the case in the days of Simmel and even at the present time?

Answering this question requires referring to the 20th century. What happened during this time that was so special compared to other periods in history? It was *special* indeed: The emperor in China, the Tsar in Russia, and the emperor in Germany disappeared in revolutions; World War I brought death and destruction to Europe; Japan occupied large parts of China and maltreated millions of noncombatant Chinese citizens; Stalin, Hitler, and Mao Zedong became dictators; the German Nazi regime killed millions of

European Jews; World War II exceeded even the horrors of World War I; America deposited atom bombs on Hiroshima and Nagasaki in Japan; communist regimes tortured, deported, and killed millions of dissenters in numerous countries; China went through several phases of this madness, culminating in the "cultural revolution"; then there was the Korean war and the war in Vietnam; and this list, alas, is far from complete. How can a humankind with this recent history be self-confident, let alone proud of itself? How can the educated individual today, as participant in the world-wide collective conscience of these events, avert deep-seated fears?

Of course, Simmel could not know about these facts, but he very likely saw something of this nature coming when he died at the end of World War I in 1918. He observed and predicted what in sociology later was referred to as *secularization,* but he also acknowledged that the need of humans for a religious orientation will not disappear even when traditional religions no longer find acceptance as they did over centuries. Simmel frequently makes his point using striking comparisons. He likens a religious person to a person in love:

> Just as an erotic person is always erotic in character, whether or not he has created—or ever will create—an object of love, so too is a religious person always religious, whether or not he believes in a god. (Simmel, 1997, p. 5)

Simmel sees in personal religiousness a potential for interpreting life and the world in a certain way. This potential is part of the human condition, and different cultures have responded to it in different ways, but all cultures have developed their peculiar kind of religion as a response. "Religiousness thus can be seen in this light: as a form according to which the human soul experiences life and comprehends its existence" (Simmel, 1997, p. 5). Simmel returns to his initial rejection of the idea that problems people have with religions may be the result of progress in scientific knowledge. This, to him, is completely erroneous. He states that "there clearly can be no conflict whatever between religiosity and science" (Simmel, 1997, p. 5). Such conflict cannot come about because they each—in their own way—are interpretations and representations of life and the world *in its entirety.*

Thus, religion and science do not talk about different subjects, but they report on the same overall conditions in different ways. Therefore, there can be no conflict between any one of the sciences and the humanities, just as there can be no conflict between scientific knowledge and religious knowledge. However, Simmel concedes that the *scientific style* of thinking, the attitude that he refers to as "scientific criticism," may well destroy certain foundations for religious faith. I mentioned above that the criterion for *what is real* has changed; the quality of truth has become attributed to personal and individual experience in a laboratory.

How to Restore the Acceptance of Religions

Remarkably, Simmel (1997) does not leave it at a sociological analysis but has the courage to make concrete recommendations for how the acceptance of religions can be restored. In his view, the religious bodies, the churches and similar teaching authorities in charge of propagating whatever faith they represent, should "leave the transcendental world of ideas" that these institutions have created for themselves (p. 6). This is, of course, a highly controversial suggestion. The reason Simmel sees that departure as necessary is this: The *religions* must move closer to the *religious*, even though Simmel himself does not word it this way.

Simmel (1997) does write, however, that he hopes to see the religions

> returning to those unique impulses of life itself which are to the religious person the essence of his being, the intrinsic coloring and form of all his inner and outer existence. . . . If religion is not a set of claims but a certain state of being—which is precisely what enables it to interpret and judge empirical phenomena—then it can be no more disproved by science than can any other state of being. It becomes refutable, however, as soon as its representative images become detached from this inner essence and instead become rigidified into a system of knowledge that somehow imitates the thought processes of science and thus is compelled to compete with the latter on its own terms. (p. 6)

This is the view Simmel expressed in 1909.

In 1918, the year of his death, Simmel published a less optimistic account of the condition of religion. It is included in a longer article titled "The Conflict of Modern Culture" (Simmel, 1997, pp. 20–25). The solution he hopes for in 1918 is for religiosity to become a direct process of life, as in mysticism. In the past, Simmel writes, there appeared in history the periodic need to replace outmoded forms of religious belief with new ones. This became necessary because the old forms "gradually stiffen[ed] into superficialities and narrowness" (p. 21). The successive replacement of obsolete forms by renewed ones seemed to have worked in the past. But now it seems doubtful to Simmel whether renewal can continue along that path. Therefore, he hopes for inspiration from a famous mystic: "Angelus Silesius gives us a foretaste by using those remnants of form which mysticism supplies" (p. 22). The objects of religiosity in mysticism are no longer specific, sacred things or texts or rituals; they are the qualities of life itself. Simmel quotes the mystic's own words: "The saint when he is drinking / Is just as pleasing to God / As if he were praying and singing" (p. 22).

Drinking, eating, working while living the daily life of a religious person in the face of the sacred—such a form of pure being might be the future of religion, rather than the acknowledgment of this or that prescribed action or thing to be worshipped. This vision must not be misunderstood as promoting "secular religion." Rather, the closeness to the beyond is given as "a direct process of life, encompassing every pulse beat" (Simmel, 1997, p. 22). Accordingly, religiosity as mysticism is a form of "being," not of "having"; it is merely *a way of life* because it does not deal with objects (p. 22).

Simmel (1997) summarizes that idea of a possible future of religiosity in a sentence that he calls paradoxical: "The soul wants to keep its faithful quality, although it has lost faith in all determined and predetermined religious content" (p. 22). But Simmel then acknowledges that this is an illusion. Cultural change and intellectual development can steal the clothing in which religiosity is covered but cannot take religion's life (p. 23). And there is no reason to assume that religion can then continue to exist, as it were, naked: New "clothing" will be found and given it.

Therefore a "formless" and naked religiosity can only be a mental interlude because its "nakedness" signifies that it is contained in life itself. But life cannot be a form; it requires form to be lived. This is reminiscent of the tension between charisma and institutionalization in the writings of Max Weber (1920/2013): The admirable and often adored quality of a charismatic person is so vulnerable that it needs the protection that only an institution can grant. On the other hand, any institution entails the danger of leading away from the meaning it was designed to protect and to hand on to the next generation. This contradiction can be illustrated by numerous examples in the history of culture.

Simmel's reflections have led to questions of the philosophy of religion and of the psychology of religion. In order to return to the sociology of religion, we should take a look at what we have already learned from Simmel: Sociology is about relationships, and in the case of religion, what we are dealing with are relationships between a mortal (who knows he or she will die sometime) and an immortal (who is believed to be eternal because there is no death). It is then a necessary quality of religious relationships to have no time limit. This is the requirement of being eternal.

But in modern society there is change, and religions cannot escape the necessity to also change. So, in Simmel's terminology, the content (what we would like to believe) must be eternally unchanged to be credible, but the form in which it is presented and communicated from generation to generation must be flexible to be current and therefore also credible. This is the contradiction that unavoidably seems to be inherent in the way religion works, if it does, today. Alas, this contradiction besets not only religion but, as we shall see, other areas of social life, like marriage and the family.

Conclusion

The sociology of religion needs a definition of its area of research: Religion is a system of beliefs that defines life after death as real. It is not within the scope and ability of sociology to determine whether religious statements about the beyond are true or not. This question must be left open. However, to the believer and follower of a religion, the statements of faith must be true, must relate to something real, and must be based on personal relationships with one or several immortal persons that are eternal.

The discoveries of modern science cannot be blamed for the weaknesses in religious faith in recent times. But the way of thinking that comes with science leads to defining as *believable reality* only what can be proven in a laboratory experiment. Simmel asks how the acceptance of religion can be restored. He suggests that the established religions leave their respective transcendental worlds of ideas and instead observe the unique impulses of life itself. Simmel thinks intellectual development can rob religion of its clothing but cannot take religion's life. A new form will be found for religiosity as one of life's basic contents.

Simmel's unusual approach to religion raises a number of questions:

- Is it really convincing to define and recognize a belief system as a religion independently of what the content of faith happens to be?
- If relations with a god or other immortal are endowed with the quality of being eternal, then how can any change or development in the context of that religion be justified?
- What does Simmel mean when he writes that religion can be robbed of its clothing but not of its life?
- How can a contemporary religion observe the unique impulses of life itself?

5

Evolution

The Family and Private Life

The Bond Between Mother and Child

In order to get an impression of how Simmel approached the topic of evolution of family life, we will take a look at his article "Toward a Sociology of the Family," which appeared in 1895 in two consecutive weekend editions of a German daily newspaper (Simmel, 1895b). His overriding methodological interest is the evolution of culture. In this text, he addresses the then-new and, in many respects, sensational findings of cultural anthropology on how family life and sexual relations were conducted in native tribal societies.

Some writers constructed an evolutionary theory that assumed that in an early stage of human development, there were various forms of polygamy and even promiscuity. Against that notion, Simmel (1895b) points to the well-known fact that some species of birds are monogamous: One female and one male stay together, assist each other, and help bring up their offspring together until one of them dies (p. 6). Looking at these birds seems to leave no doubt that monogamy can be regarded as natural. But to study animal behavior and then draw conclusions from that for human beings is highly problematic because the comparison frequently does not take into consideration the vast difference between animal life guided by instincts and human conduct determined by the voluntary adoption of ethical rules.

Simmel (1895b) explains the remarkable varieties in family cultures as being the result of specific historical circumstances and necessities to adapt to different long-term living conditions. Nowhere does Simmel see a basis for deducing an imagined state of original human family life from what has been observed and reported by cultural anthropologists (p. 8). When, nevertheless, such speculations appear in the literature, they can be explained by the inclination of the human mind to create unity out of the diversity of observations and thus transform the disparity of historical phenomena into a hypothetical shared prehistoric beginning, as is also expressed in the creation myths of religions.

Looking, nevertheless, for common foundations shared by all family cultures, Simmel (1895b) has no doubt that the firm center around which different forms of family organization have grown in the course of cultural evolution is not the union between two adult humans but the bond between mother and child (p. 8). The mother-child dyad is the firm hub around which the ups and downs of married life revolve. It is essentially the same at all times and in any culture, whereas marriage takes on different forms in different regions and in different eras. With this in mind, Simmel points to anthropological data that show that the position of the father is not the same in every culture. The closeness of the mother to her child is a given, regardless of how other relations are institutionalized in the family, but how close or distant the father is to his offspring varies considerably.

The notion of biological fatherhood as the powerful source of a feeling of belonging and authority, which has evolved in the Judeo-Christian and other patrilineal traditions as the foundation for emotional closeness, cannot be generalized; it is, to Simmel, a special and even unusual development. The male caretaker of a young child felt close to the infant in various cultures on different grounds. The child was his to look after, protect, and bring up independently of who the biological begetter was. He felt responsible on account of his closeness to the child's mother.

Simmel (1895b) points out that in less-developed cultures, men are eager to bring their women, who in some cases are their sisters, into contact with the chief, the priest, or other prominent man. They believe that any child born out of such a contact—who then would nevertheless be taken care of by the man—would inherit the admired qualities of his or her noble begetter. This would later benefit the whole family (p. 10). Accordingly, the concept of "father" must have undergone a long and complicated process of development. In the course of that, it changed from (a) relating to the child merely via its mother, who was close to the man helping to take care of the infant, to (b) a "direct and individual relationship between the begetter and the child" (p. 10).

Simmel introduces a distinction between two ways of relating to the next generation; this can occur by handing on material goods as valued possessions or by passing on genetic information via blood relations. Of course, the two can be combined, but Simmel assumes that in the distant cultural past, the former may have been a powerful motif standing on its own. Therefore, knowing who the begetter of a person was did not have any relevance because blood relations between the adult male and the male child in his care did not matter much; it had no consequences for inheriting property. They were close to each other on grounds other than one being the begetter of the other, and that closeness on different grounds resulted in the younger being the heir of the older. As soon, however, as passing on wealth was tied to blood, the notion of being a "father" became crucial and was necessarily filled with a new and different meaning.

In order to know without doubt who the father as begetter was, the respective clans needed to insist on the faithfulness of the wives during marriage and on their virginity prior to it (Simmel, 1895b, p. 10). The unconditional limitation to having sexual relations only with the spouse thus developed earlier on the side of the women, and only there does Simmel see it founded in the principle of inheriting wealth according to blood bonds. The demand for the husband to be faithful as well was a later and much slower development, which, according to Simmel, rests on different foundations.

Simmel assumes that one of the driving forces in this direction was the call for equal rights for women, which resulted in subjecting men to the same limitations that women were already compelled to observe. As a result, men eventually agreed to letting themselves be governed by the same rules that they had imposed on their women, even though the considerations that originally led to the requirement of faithfulness did not apply to them. Simmel also concedes that, obviously, there are a number of other reasons for being faithful in marriage.

Erotic love of one spouse for the other is a source of marital faithfulness. Simmel (1895b) mentions that in modern societies, according to widespread expectations, such love is the foundation of marriage. It is seen as determining the way a marriage develops and the quality it attains. In his article he also voices the opinion that originally love was not the precondition but—hopefully—the consequence of marriage (p. 11). The marriage bond was based on a number of considerations, partly economic and partly political, in the sense of establishing or reaffirming bonds between clans. This is still the case today in many parts of the world. The young couple was—and is—then expected to fall in love after they get married.

One reason for the victory of the principle of monogamy was, for Simmel, the democratic ideal of equality for all: Because the number of female and male humans is about equal, it follows that each of them should be married to one and not to several humans of the other gender. Therefore, under the regime of democracy, all men must agree that each of them is entitled to one woman only. Also in this context, Simmel's attention shifts back to his evolutionary interest: A monogamous marriage results in an educational situation in the family that he assumes to be superior to any other for the development of the children.

As a result, the next generation will be superior to children from the previous one who were raised under different conditions. If they grow up in a group in which the parents could not unite their efforts in bringing up their common offspring, then those children will have less favorable chances for developing. Monogamous marriage thus entails an evolutionary advantage comparable to more fertile soil or more advanced agricultural technology. Consequently, the struggle for survival will make it more likely that the monogamous two-parents group will outlast other family cultures in which the mother is more or less left alone to take care of her offspring (Simmel, 1895b, p. 13).

Evolution and the Rule of Reversal

Simmel (1895b) generalizes a rule of reversal in his analysis of family evolution: At first, people are joined in marriage by their respective relatives, and personal love will result as a consequence of their marital union. Then, later in the evolution of family cultures, this sequence is reversed and marriage is expected to follow from the fact that a couple has fallen in love. Similarly, at first the necessity to produce a next generation of young people led to marriage. Then that, too, was reversed: Having children was seen as the consequence of getting married. Simmel observes that what these two reversals have in common is they both began with the interests of the group having priority and led to individual interests becoming more and more dominant. But social obligations do not disappear; they shift, as it were, from the generation of grandparents, who under the old regime initiate the marriage, to the coming generation, whose care and upbringing now becomes central as the result of the marriage and the duty of the couple (p. 14).

There is yet a third case for the rule of reversal that draws Simmel's attention. It relates to the way economic and emotional conditions influence each other in marital arrangements. This leads to the topic of money, a phenomenon about which Simmel later was to write a whole book. We shall deal with that in Chapter 6. Just as it is one-sided to try to explain everything from the perspective of the economy, as if money were the only thing that counts, it is also one-sided to pretend that money does not matter in the life of a family. Indeed, often marriages are contracted expressly on economic conditions, and in many indigenous cultures, money must be paid in the event of marriage.

For instance, on a low level of subsistence, every adult member of a family is crucial as a farm hand who contributes to producing the food needed. If a young woman gets married and, as a consequence, shifts membership from her family of origin to the family of her future husband, then in economic terms, it means hiring away a crucial part of the work force. It makes sense if that loss is compensated by paying a certain amount of money to the family of the bride. It may seem like purchasing her, but that is too narrow a view of what goes on economically.

Having clarified this, we now come back to the rule of reversal. At first, the bride is seen as an economic asset that must be evaluated in money and paid for, but then, in a slightly more advanced stage of evolution, she is appreciated very much because she was so expensive. This reads as ridiculous at first because it is reminiscent of purchasing an automobile and then holding it in high esteem. Simmel explains this reversal: Coming up with the required amount of money to pay for the bride requires considerable sacrifice on the part of the groom and his family. Consequently, it is likely that what has been acquired as the result of making a sacrifice will be considered valuable. Simmel cites the example of a mother who makes innumerable sacrifices for her small child and, as a result, is very vitally attached to it in motherly love. Similarly, the groom who had to save and toil for years to finally be able to "afford" a bride will be determined to consider her "valuable."

In imperial Germany in Simmel's days, the husband was bound by law to support his wife financially throughout her life. Simmel mentions that this would add up to a sizable amount over the years, and strange as that may seem, he believes that it has contributed to improving the social position of women in society. Therefore, in Simmel's view, the sacrifice that was required of the groom in an early phase of cultural evolution has set the stage for a gradual elevation of the social position of the woman.

The Status of Women in a Future Society

The status of women in a future society is also the topic in Simmel's (1890b) text "Toward a Psychology of Women." Much of the paper reads like boys' talk due to the fact that it addresses an all-male audience, referring to males as "we." Toward the end of the paper, he describes how a woman can be coquettish and how it is part of the secret tied to that way to behave that the goal is not actual seduction but merely, as it were, faking that goal. Then he goes on:

> Knowing full well that being coquettish is not serious gives us a certain confidence which causes us to yield to her charm to a large extent; that we would not be able to do if we knew that the path upon which we have entered were to lead to the end. (Simmel, 1890b, p. 17)

Simmel's sophisticated language means we would not flirt with the girl unless we could be sure that she does not want to go "all the way."

Anyone who has ever prepared a presentation knows that in an oral delivery, the content must be geared to the expected audience, and if later taken out of context, some remarks may not sound as plausible as they may have sounded to the original listeners. This, plus the fact that Simmel wrote this more than a century ago, must give us pause in judging it. But there are several insights developed in the paper that may be useful even today. Simmel sees human males as having progressed to a more advanced stage in evolution than women. Today this reads like an insult to females. Simmel, however, draws the conclusion that (a) if someone charges ahead, it does not mean that he or she is more competent, nor does it preclude that others follow him; and (b) women have more potential for further development in the future and will still be creative when males run out of steam because they started early.

> For since we frequently imagine that she has not evolved completely, we simply sense that beyond what is obvious about her there must be something else that has not taken shape; we sense that in the background of what she is able to give there is something deeper. (Simmel, 1890b, p. 19)

Like it or not, this is the way Simmel saw women in 1890: Women are underdeveloped! But then, who wants to be fully developed if it means nothing more, nothing new, and nothing exciting can be expected of him or her? Maybe this applies to nations as it does to persons. Simmel values potential more highly than achievement, and he admires women precisely because of their unrealized potential.

This is seen in the context of his observation that there is interdependence between individualization (in Simmel's view, more advanced among males) and the width of the social circle in which the person interacts. A narrow social environment, limited maybe to relatives and neighbors, will hinder the development of a differentiated individual. It will, on the other hand, supply more protection and emotional support than a wider circle is able to give. The latter will confront the person with more competition and thus force him or her toward more specialization and self-sufficiency. In 1890, Simmel (1890b) correctly sees women more located in the narrow circle and males more in the wider ones (p. 8). This was no doubt true in Germany then. Looking at today's gender debates it means this: Access to organizations and institutions of the "wider circle" is not simply a matter of money making but, according to Simmel, also of personal development for women as well as for males.

An additional topic next to the interdependence between individualization and scope of social circle is the idea of an inter-gender division of labor. Using the method of evolutionism, trying to explain culture and society in terms of change and development, Simmel assumes that a division of labor as the basis for the chance to cooperate is needed not merely between individuals but also between groups of persons. He explores the development of cooperation between females and males as a historical given that apparently no culture can do without, provided it does not want to put its own survival into question. Simmel believes one of the reasons males, himself included, appreciate women is the fact that they are different from males.

This is not meant as the superficial statement it seems to be at first glance. Human beings in general value highly what they themselves lack but find present in another person. Not wanting to admit how far each individual is from being perfect, humans are fascinated by the notion of coming close to perfection if united with another because then they together compensate for what appeared to be missing. This gives rise to the belief that if we were to join forces, or rather our special abilities, we would be nearly perfect together.

Simmel (1890b) points out that this concept of joining forces can be followed on the individual level of person to person as well as on the group level of gender to gender. But a precondition for this concept is, of course, that there are differences between women and men (p. 11). On the macro level, then, society will be closer to perfection if the special potentials of the male group on the one hand and the female group on the other are merged.

Finally, Simmel addresses differentiation and specialization *within* the female population. Because Simmel expects that social evolution will have its effect on women with a certain time lag as compared to men, individualization and specialization will have more striking consequences among females in the foreseeable future than among males. But he also assumes that the biological facts of pregnancy, childbirth, and infant care will cause the evolutionary path of the women not only to be delayed but also to proceed through unfamiliar territory, in comparison to what the males have gone through.

Simmel predicts that the push by more and more women to leave the narrow circle of family life and neighborhood in order to become modern will be achieved at the expense of other, less advanced women in the same society. Those, he assumed, will be pushed back into the traditional milieu of the household even more forcefully. This may reemphasize class barriers by delegating childbearing to the lower classes. Indeed, the original meaning of the word *proletariat* was "those who have offspring." Simmel (1890b) writes that the evolution within the female segment of the population will create woman academics on the one hand and mothers, cooks, and housekeepers on the other. He brings this unpopular insight to the attention of the sociologists of gender: One group of women may have to make the sacrifice in order to enable the other group of women to modernize (p. 12).

The Demise of the Patriarchal Household

In his book of 1908, Simmel (1908/2009) frequently refers to the family, even though there is no specific chapter on that topic. Anthony Blasi (2010) has recently pointed to the significance of those passages. Simmel (1908/2009) mentions that the traditional family household, which existed in many highly developed agrarian cultures and which in his text he calls patriarchal, "always numbers twenty to thirty people" (p. 75). The living conditions and environmental influences vary greatly among the agrarian cultures. Accordingly, those cannot be the cause for the striking similarity in size. Simmel therefore assumes "that the internal interactions that constitute the particular structure of the household generate the necessary proportions of narrowness and width" in this family type to secure its stable existence over long periods of time (p. 75). He thus sees internal needs as the reason for keeping membership within a certain range.

Next, Simmel describes that family in more detail. It can be typified not merely by its size but also by the high degree of "intimacy and solidarity" among its members, as well as by the type of leadership within it: One male father figure rules the group in a way that is referred to as paternalism (from the Latin *pater*, meaning father). That included the patriarch's control over each individual's personal affairs in order to bring them in line with the interests of the group as well as with his own interests. Family interest plus the desired intimacy and solidarity led to the maximum membership of about 30 persons.

The paternalistic style of leadership would not make a successful integration of a larger number likely. And the need of the family for conferring its unique notion of identity on each of its members, for experiencing religious unity as a small congregation, for defending itself effectively and maintaining its family pride, all that together required a minimum number of members, no less than about 20. Thus there were certain formal, numerical require-ments for maintaining a given family culture.

As Simmel teaches consistently throughout his career, individualization as the evolution of a modern and more differentiated person can happen only in wider company. Thus on the threshold of modernity the person could no longer be fenced into the patriarchal family household, and as a result, the social group of origin exploded and imploded at the same time: The "wider company" could not be provided in the household, so its members were beginning to leave it. This coincided with leaving the countryside and con-verting to city life.

At the same time, while individualization set in, the longing for intimacy increased more and more. That new need for privacy and very personal close-ness, however, required a small family of fewer than 10 members. As the fam-ily is torn apart into a wider and a narrower circle, we see at the same time societies torn apart into a private world and a public world. The modern person must thus learn how to behave in both spheres. Nobody has the option of choosing between the two, for under the condition of modernity, the person needs to be able to act confidently as a private person as well as in public life.

Simmel (1908/2009) also reflects on types of marriages (pp. 80–106). He sees in some marriages the unresolved confrontation between the desire to be closer and the insistence on keeping a distance. If there can be no loving compromise between the two, the feeling of being "internally estranged" results in not wanting a child because its presence would make the experi-ence of estrangement even more painful (p. 87). Yet marriages characterized by passion and exceptional erotic closeness may also lead to not wanting a child because the child causes distance between the high flying lovers and brings them down to earth to their roles of parents.

Marriage as a Special Dyad

Marriage also fascinates Simmel because he sees in it the exception to the rule that *dyads* (stable relationships between two persons) are nothing but the sum of what the two persons have to contribute. Because this is normally so, as a rule a group has a minimum of three members. As long as there is nothing "supra-personal" that would persist even if one of the members were replaced by somebody else, it would be nonsensical to even speak about a two-person group. But marriage is different and special! It is not simply like any other dyad. Simmel (1908/2009) observes that "there are decidedly poor marriages between admirable personalities and very good ones between quite deficient individuals" (p. 87).

To explain that, Simmel (1908/2009) states that a marriage as it is lived in real life "can have a character that coincides with no member" (p. 87). A disciplined spouse can be aware of his or her deficiencies, yet carefully keep them from entering into the marital relationship. Instead, the spouse succeeds in contributing the very best components of his or her personality as husband or wife. Thus marriage is an exceptional case that cannot be subsumed to the general rules that apply to "the basic 'I' and 'Thou'" (p. 88).

This requires more explanation: Why can this be so? The first reason Simmel (1908/2009) mentions is the "incomparable closeness" that is unique to married life. He believes that "the egoism of the individual is so fundamentally overridden not only in favor of the other but in favor of the relationship as a whole, which includes family interests, family honor, the children above all" that conditions can result that would not be achieved in any other dyad (p. 88). A second reason is the decisive role of a "third person"—the person who arranged the first contact between the future spouses, or who worked out the economic and financial framework for the marriage, or who was the religious leader or government bureaucrat who certified that the two have entered into a marital bond. This institutionalized involvement of the larger social context indicates "the sociologically unique structure of marriage" (p. 88).

After the quality of special closeness and the role of the third person, there is a third reason why marriage is different from other dyads: It is a remarkable realization of the contradiction between individual freedom and collective control. On the one hand, of course, a couple experiences the privacy of marital life free from social interference, but on the other hand, the community will intervene immediately in case of marital offenses or child abuse. If close friends enter into a fist fight, it is largely considered their personal affair, but if fighting breaks out in a marriage, the public will react and consider it a provocation. Therefore, Simmel believes that in no other social relationship is the closeness between the contradictory conditions—personal freedom and public control—so obvious.

Simmel (1908/2009) likes to argue such contradictions are united in real life and finds a fourth reason for treating marriage as special: The sexual act in marriage is utterly private and personal, but at the same time, it is being performed in the collective service of the human species as potential procreation. This enormous tension created by that contradiction requires its institutionalization as marriage. It also follows from this reflection that marriage can never be merely a sexual relationship; it must be more than that (p. 90).

In his chapter on conflict, Simmel (1908/2009) deals with a type of fighting that may occur among married partners due to jealousy (pp. 256–258). He analyzes the psychological conditions of this emotion and gives relationships beset by jealousy little chance of recovery. The spouse or lover who believes to have reason for being jealous can only point to having a right to be loved. However, Simmel writes, "to desire to enforce [love] with a mere right, however deeply and well deserved it may be in various ways, is as senseless as wanting to order a bird, who is long gone out of earshot and eyesight, back into its cage" (p. 257).

All this makes marriage a complicated and sociologically interesting subject. The institution on which the union of husband and wife is based in almost all cultures at their advanced stages of evolution depends for its success on the continued presence of erotic love. That is a component that cannot be commanded and the presence of which in a marriage cannot be ensured by appealing to a sense of duty and respect for rights. Simmel (1908/2009) illustrates this point further:

> This ineffectiveness of entitlement in matters of love generates the phenomenon characteristic of jealousy: that in the end it clings to the external proofs of the feeling, which are indeed enforceable by the appeal to the sense of duty, yet guarding . . . the body of the relationship as if it still had something of its soul in it. (p. 257)

And indeed, that is the impression one gets of certain marriages, that they sadly have become bodies with no souls in them.

In the last book Simmel published prior to his death, he also refers to the sexual act and points to what it has in common with dying. He sees a deep similarity between the acts of procreation and of dying as central catastrophes of life. Again, as in the context of marriage, he points to the frightening identity of what is simultaneously an extreme personal experience and an act performed in the name of the human species. Dying and begetting, Simmel (1918) states, have this in common (p. 21).

Conclusion

Chapter 5 presents Simmel's ideas on private life and on women. Research findings from cultural anthropology and comparative family studies have shown that a variety of family types exist, but what they all have in common, in Simmel's view, is the mother-child dyad as their center. Biological fatherhood is seen by him as a late development in the evolution of culture. It became important only at the time when material goods were handed down to the next generation according to blood relationship. Simmel sees monogamy as having an evolutionary advantage because it produces a better educational situation for the offspring than other family types do.

Simmel explains changes following his rule of reversal: At first, marriage arrangements made by family members precede romantic love, then that is reversed. At first, the need for offspring leads to marriage; later, people get married and then decide to have children. In less developed cultures, the groom pays a price to gain his wife; later, the fact that the wife is obtained as the result of major sacrifices raises her value in the eyes of her husband. Simmel also looks at the division of labor between genders, first on the individual level between one woman and one man, then on the group level between all women and all men of one society as the two gender groups confront each other, and finally on the division of labor within the group of women: Some of them become academics; others are left behind.

Finally in this chapter, Simmel explains why the demise of the patriarchal household is unavoidable. Then he describes the uniqueness of marriage in comparison to all the other dyads. It is based on the quality of special closeness in married life, on the role of the "third person," and on the contradiction between individual freedom and collective control. On the one hand, a couple experiences the privacy of its marital life as free from social interference, but on the other hand, the community will intervene immediately in case of marital offenses or child abuse. Simmel describes the psychological conditions of jealousy and gives relationships beset by this emotion little chance of recovery.

A discussion of this chapter can be based on the following questions:

- Is the idea that fatherhood has been a relatively late development in cultural history far-fetched? If not, how can it be proven?
- Why does Simmel believe that monogamy is good for small children?
- When Simmel makes the statement that in his day women are less developed than men, how does he evaluate that state of affairs, assuming it was described correctly?
- Why does Simmel see no chance for recovery if a relationship is beset with jealousy?

6

Equality Versus Liberty

Competition and Money

Competition as an Indirect Form of Fighting

When Simmel writes about family life, his statements should be seen in the context of society and of sociology as the new discipline designed to study society: Marriage and the family, gender relations, and human sexuality must be investigated to understand society better. The same is true when he writes about competition and money. What do these phenomena mean, how do they work in the larger context of society, and how do they contribute to social development?

Competition is, to Simmel, a civilized form of conflict. He discusses that topic against the background of how types of human conflict evolve. Under less-developed conditions, conflict is closer to fighting, with the goal—at the lowest level—of killing the adversary. Then, as cultural evolution sets in, the goal becomes more benign: maybe not exactly kill him, but give him a beating, then use him as a slave. On the next higher step, it will suffice to merely threaten him, and eventually there will be competition. This is, admittedly, a somewhat humorous way of summarizing Simmel's ideas on the evolution of conflict. But it is true that he considers competition a highly cultivated form of indirect fighting.

This raises the question why there should be any conflict in society at all. Could not all human persons simply be kind to each other and treat each other with love, or at least respect, and forego any type of fighting? Simmel is familiar with this dream of eternal and complete peace, but he does not think it can work. As we have seen repeatedly in this text, his social thought hinges on the notion of evolution, not biological, as in the theory of Charles Darwin, but cultural evolution. Both concepts assume that there will be a process of selection or, as it is frequently referred to, of survival of the fittest. In the case of biological evolution, this applies to physical characteristic of the individual representative of a species. In the case of cultural evolution, it applies primarily to groups and to whole societies, not so much with regard to their physical properties but with regard to their cultural achievements, such as ethics, philosophy, religion, government, and, indeed, military technology.

If there were no conflict at all, then how could the more advanced be selected over the backward types? Because, according to this line of reasoning, some type of conflict is necessary, Simmel asks the question, "Which is the best available form of conflict?" His answer is competition. But competition—like other results achieved slowly though cultural evolution—is always beset with the danger of reverting back to an earlier stage that seemed to have been overcome. If someone beats up his or her competitor, then according to Simmel what goes on between them no longer qualifies as competition; it has gone back to a lower level conflict, a physical fight.

What, according to Simmel, is so special about competition is not merely that this high level form of conflict does less damage to the participants; it even produces downright advantages to other people who are not even directly involved in the confrontation of the two or more competitors. The general public profits from competition because this form of conflict results in better quality and lower prices for the goods and services that become available on the market. Thus Simmel includes this positive effect on non-combatants in his definition of competition: Unless a form of conflict results in some benefit for all and thus promotes the common good, it is not—to Simmel—competition. He describes it as "a form of struggle fought by means of objective performances, to the advantage of a third person," that third person usually being the customer (Simmel, 1903b, p. 1021).

Having clarified what he means by competition, Simmel distinguishes between two types of this form of indirect conflict. The first is one step away from physical confrontation: It does not suffice to be the winner if one wishes to decide the confrontation in one's own favor by somehow defeating one's opponent. What matters is, in addition, to win the approval of the customer or other audience who witnessed the struggle between the competitors.

> Competition of this kind is distinctly colored by the fact that the outcome of the fight in no way fulfils the purpose of the fight, as would apply to all those cases in which fighting is motivated by rage or revenge, punishment or victory as an . . . end in itself. (Simmel, 1903b, p. 1010)

Thus, in this first type, competition already includes additional persons beyond the two or more competing opponents.

The second type of competition may be seen as another step further removed from direct fighting. Here no one aims his or her force or energy against his opponent; he or she tries to deploy the best possible abilities while—on the surface—ignoring the competing party. This means from the perspective of society as a whole, no energy is wasted and no mindless destruction is committed. Maximizing one's efforts is motivated, however, by

> the mutual awareness of the opponent's performance; and yet, if observed from the outside, seems to proceed as if there were no adversary present in this world, but merely the goal . . . . One fights the opponent without turning against him—without touching him, so to speak. (Simmel, 1903b, p. 1010)

This second type, then, is competition in its fully developed form.

Simmel (1903b) describes the various benefits by pointing out that "the goal of competition between parties in society is nearly always to attain the approval of one or several third persons" (p. 1012). It is achieved in part by

> this incredible effect of socializing people: it compels the competitor, who finds his fellow competitor at his side and only as a result of that really starts competing, to approach and appeal to the potential customer, to connect to him, to find out his weaknesses and strengths and to adapt to them, to find or to build all imaginable bridges that might tie the producer's existence and performance to the potential customer. . . . The antagonistic tension against the competitor sharpens the merchant's sense for the inclinations of the public into an almost clairvoyant instinct for coming changes in taste, in fashion, in interests. (p. 1012)

It is this socializing effect of competition that actually educates competing people.

Society, therefore, depends on the functioning of competition. Some so-called socialist countries under communist rule have gone through a phase in their history when competition was banned because it appeared to be contrary to the notion of the universal brotherhood of the working class. The undesired effect was, however, that those countries did not develop well during that time. Simmel suggests that governments have a duty not to hinder but to protect competition so it can survive any attacks against it. Defending competition against those who wish to combat it because, according to them, it is against the principle of universal brotherhood is not the only task of governments, according to Simmel.

In addition, governments are required to purify competition by making certain tools and practices illegal. This brings Simmel (1903b) "to the formation of cartels . . . a point at which companies are organized no longer for fighting for a share of the market, but rather for supplying the market according to a joint plan" (p. 1019). He explains the difference between the guilds and cartels. He also mentions a simple criterion for outlawing certain agreements between competitors and argues that "achieving complete control of the market results in making the consumer dependent and, as a consequence, in making competition as such superfluous" and even impossible to implement (p. 1019).

Simmel (1903b) expects governments and ethical imperatives as supplied by religious or political groups to purify competition by eliminating components that are not essential to it. He also expects them to contribute to modern society by leaving competition intact and by guaranteeing "its continued existence" (p. 1019). It is Simmel's considered opinion that "society does not want to do without the advantages that competition between individuals entails for it, which by far exceed the disadvantages it incurs by the occasional annihilation of individuals in the course of competition" (p. 1020). This reference to "annihilation" sounds frightening; however, what Simmel means is the destruction of their businesses, not their lives. For competition to be able to function in society, it needs to be governed by proscriptions that originate from legal as well as moral sources (p. 1022).

Humans Are Equal Before the Law

As the title of this chapter suggests, Simmel combines this evolutionary typology of conflict with the contradiction that often appears in society between equality and liberty. Obviously, for competition to work, society needs to give all competitors equal opportunity when they start competing. But after competition has been in effect for some time, one of the competitors will have outsold the others, will have become more wealthy, and will possibly have even thrown one or several others out of the market. As a consequence, they may have started out as equals, but given the liberty they need to do their best, they end up quite unequal. The same applies outside the economy: The law in modern developed societies must treat all citizens the same; they must be equal before the law. But confronted with the law, one person may go to jail while another may be exonerated.

As was mentioned at the end of Chapter 1, to tell people that liberty and equality can be developed in politics in a way that will arrive at a friction-free alignment of the two is, to Simmel, an opportunistic lie. This is so because if a political system insists on equality in the form of the approximate sameness of material living conditions, it has no choice but to enforce that by taking away liberty, at least from a certain segment of its population. What we then get as a result is equality without liberty. If, on the other hand, as in the United States at the present time, there is no limit to how wealthy an individual may become, we see a striking degree of inequality evolve under the conditions of unlimited (economic) liberty. This alternative is clearly liberty without equality.

It was, according to Simmel, the erroneous notion that humans were and are equal by nature that started the confrontation between equality and liberty on the wrong foot. To assume—or even dogmatically decree—that in a remote early state of natural conditions all humans were equal was, to Simmel, an error of devastating proportions. By contrast, Simmel (1949) states that in the absence of culture, naked nature—if a condition like that can even be imagined—would result in the most brutal form of inequality. He concludes from that more speculative observation the insight into what he calls the tragedy of individual liberty: Should it ever become a reality, it would create in its wake such dramatic inequality that it would immediately have to be revoked and suppressed (p. 313). This speculation deals with the imagined state of an all-out liberty and assigns it the consequence of unbearable inequality.

Simmel, looking at this contradiction from a historical perspective, compares the cry for equality to a pair of crutches on which the demand for liberty came limping into history. Once liberty has established itself, it can throw away those crutches because it now stands on its own strong legs. Equality is now no longer needed. To apply this to competition means once competition is introduced as a principle into the economy—and not only there—it will by necessity produce more and more inequality, which as poverty or wealth hopefully will be experienced as the righteous reward for useless or useful behavior, respectively.

What Is Social About Money?

Discussing problems of inequality and thinking about poverty and wealth leads us to the topic of money. Inequality is typically measured in terms of money. Simmel spent much time and energy reflecting, lecturing, and publishing about money. Obviously, the economist is justified in studying money from the perspective of his or her discipline. But to Simmel, as a student of culture that approach is one-sided; it only picks up very limited insights about a topic having vast implications for the human condition, and thus it stays on the surface of social reality like the common statistics on inequality do.

This is so because no person can make his or her life meaningful by concentrating on economic activities alone. Being successful in business and making money in whatever way is commonly seen as a means to an end, rather than as an end in itself. Therefore, a sociology of money must find out what motivates people to be economically active and for what reasons they need money, or think they need money. It seems, then, that most persons engaged in economic activities have noneconomic motives; for example, economic success may be important for the sake of another member of the family whom that person loves, or for the sake of an acquaintance he or she wants to impress, or even for the immortal ancestors or the god he or she worships.

Although these examples of possible motives relate the economic activities to a person (a relative, a neighbor, a god), nevertheless money as the aspired reward for such work is strikingly impersonal. Simmel (1895b) believes that it is, indeed, far remote from any human individual because "it owns no qualities except its quantity" (p. 15). In addition, given its high significance in ordering the external affairs of life, money can only achieve that by staying aloof from all internal and personal values. This applies to things that are acquired in exchange for money. It does not apply to utterly personal items or deeds that have no price because they are strictly personal (p. 15).

Simmel (1907) introduces the distinction between the *material qualities* and the *meaning* of a good. The material qualities, for instance, of merchandise available in the market can be described with precision as the result of scientific analysis. Those qualities are inherent in the good in question, like its color or its weight per liter (p. 27). They do not depend on the context in which the product will have its effect, in which it will be used or consumed. However, the *meaning* of it will be ascribed to it from outside; meaning is obviously not inherent in its material makeup but is later attached like a label. It is this process of labeling that Simmel wants to investigate as giving things a value in the course of dealing with them.

With this approach to money in mind, we should not be surprised if Simmel's (1907, 1922) large book on the subject, *The Philosophy of Money,* is not about mechanisms that are active in the economy. Instead, it is primarily a reflection on what goes on between people in culture and society and how the spirit of those relationships between people is, as it were, condensed in the medium money. Simmel explains, as we shall see later, how money emerges out of interaction. In this context, he is particularly interested in two questions: (a) How is value ascribed to something? and (b) How do people manage to forget that money is only valuable because it was ascribed value and not because it is valuable in itself?

The isolated individual, of course, can excuse himself or herself from the responsibility of having given money this or that value because it was not the effect of what one person did. But society as a whole is constantly giving money value or devaluating it. Yet, this process is neither recognized nor acknowledged, and the value of money is typically seen as being the result of a number of different technical economic causes, but it is to Simmel the result of social definition or social construction. Simmel considers this phenomenon to be a striking case of alienation, according to the original meaning of the word in Latin (conferring property rights from one owner to another owner), because the members participating in the economy assign a certain value to their money but then refuse to admit that they did it.

In order to shed more light on this strange, and in a way to Simmel scandalous, condition, he sets out to explain the process of value attribution. It is something that goes on between a person and a thing, and the thing may become valuable because it seems to become part of a person. If it once belonged to a famous celebrity, it will be very expensive. Wherever we draw the line between object and subject or thing and person, in contrast to color and weight, the value of a thing is in no way a quality inherent in it. The value is, to Simmel (1907), a judgment that was made about a thing, and that judgment can never be found inside the object in question; it always must be looked for in the person who finds the thing valuable or worthless and deals with it accordingly (p. 8).

The process of value attribution becomes more complex when viewed in the context of an exchange. Many relationships that appear at first sight to be exchanges of goods or services are, in fact, barter arrangements. It is more appropriate to refer to them as exchanges. Looking at it superficially, the lecturer addressing an audience, the teacher in front of his class, the journalist who hopes to reach his readers or listeners appear to be the sole producers of a performance, but in reality we are dealing in all of these cases with an exchange. These performances are produced as interactions because the performers depend on the feedback they get, or hope to get, from the people they talk to or write for (Simmel, 1907, p. 33f.).

According to his general idea of the social construction of reality, Simmel finds that humans create the objects of their observations by combining sensory impressions into what is then presented, as if they have found readymade things. They continue the process of alienation by pretending that they had nothing to do with constructing them. In the case of money, this general course of events gets pushed in a special direction: Simmel believes that humans relate to objects, some of which are closer while others are more distanced from them. He further points out that the desire to overcome the distance and to come close to the object varies. These two variables, the distance and the desire to get close, determine the value: The harder it seems to get close to something that is very desirable, the more valuable that object will appear to be for the person wanting it. Simmel thinks that this general observation even applies to a person with whom we are in love.

But even if this is true and can be corroborated in empirical research, we still are one step away from money. If we want to get something very much, we are usually prepared to make a sacrifice (Simmel, 1907, p. 31). That means we are willing to give up something in return for getting what we want. Also, the thing we want so badly is usually in the possession of another person, whom we must persuade to let us have it, short of the unacceptable idea of theft or robbery. But I can only hope to motivate that other person if I have something that he or she wants. This brings us to the evolutionary stage of a barter economy, where there need not be any money because people exchange things. So what is it that enables societies to make the step from a barter society to a money economy?

A political system in the stage of collapse, like Germany toward the end of World War II, may actually go the opposite direction; it reverts from a money economy back to a barter market, usually illegally as a so-called black market. The merchandise that took the place of money in Germany then were cigarettes. On the black market, a pound of butter was worth a certain number of cigarettes. This system had the advantage of allowing different prices to be set because the unit, one cigarette, was small. But, of course, cigarettes are not really money. If one decides not to use his cigarettes for barter, he can still smoke them. If, however, a person decides not to use his or her money as purchasing power, then there is nothing else he or she can do with it because such a decision renders it worthless.

Simmel argues like this: The distance to the desired object that needs to be overcome, plus the degree to which it is desired, results in experiencing the desired object as having a certain value. This happens on both sides of the relationship, assuming the two persons are the owners of something each other wants. If they experience what one of them has as worth just as much as what the other offers in exchange, then it is a simple one-to-one exchange. But frequently the two would agree that what one has is worth more than what the other has, so then there would be a difference.

There would be a difference in what? In price! As soon as you have a price, you potentially have money. Simmel believes that in a barter-like situation, the partners working on a deal are aware of the values of what they have and of what they want. They thus establish in their minds a sense of the value relation like this: My object is worth twice as much as your object. These relations will be separated from the goods whose comparison they originated from and will appear as an independent factor: They are given the form of money. "To put it briefly: money is the expression and means of the relationship and interdependence of people, their relativity, by which the satisfaction of one person's wishes is always mutually dependent on another person" (Simmel, 1922, p. 134).

All this works on the assumption that there are things available that people want to have. Money can only function properly if the economy achieves a healthy balance between supply and demand in the market. But in certain cases, it may become so difficult to get what one hopes to acquire, the distance between the object of desire and the person wanting it may become so enormous, that the desire is, as it were, choked. This may happen for several reasons: It may be simply too difficult to find the merchandise, or the price that one would have to pay is completely out of reach, or finally it may be in bad taste or against ethical principles to get the desired object. If this happens, the desire may degenerate into faint wishful thinking because money cannot help the person to get what he or she wants (Simmel, 1907, p. 20).

Money is the medium of the social. It is, to Simmel, the most general form of a social relationship. Due to the phenomenon of alienation, people commonly are not aware or do not want to admit what the origin of money really is: An expression of the interdependence of people as the result of a social construction. Where there is no communality, where persons in a given context do not interact as individuals with equal dignity but instead treat each other as things, money becomes meaningless. And because money does have a meaning, it must be assumed to vary significantly from culture to culture. This is a topic to be put on the research agenda in order better to understand why it is not necessarily the same thing if a government official or lawmaker in the United States accepts money as a bribe and if that happens in a less-developed society where money is still tied to a tradition of gift giving. In those countries, giving money can still, even today, be an expression of sincere interpersonal closeness.

In the West, on the other hand, money has the potential to create a welcome distance between people because it is impersonal. The employer and the wage earner can define their relationship in a contract as owing each other a certain work performance in return for a given amount of money. In addition to being under legal obligation to fulfill these terms of contract, they can stay out of each other's way. Simmel sees a clear opportunity in this to further develop individuality and personal freedom.

Conclusion

Chapter 6 deals with competition and with money. Conflict is necessary to promote evolution, and competition is desirable because it is an indirect way of fighting and because it occurs to the benefit of other people. Governments have the duty to defend competition. A precondition for competition to function well is equality of chances in the market. Simmel points out that equality and liberty cannot be combined, but rather strikingly, they turn out to be alternatives. Simmel compares the cry for equality to a pair of crutches on which the demand for liberty came limping into history.

Money is, to Simmel, the most powerful illustration of the social construction of reality. Its value is ascribed to it, but due to alienation, that definition process is not acknowledged. The value of money originates in exchange situations: Goods to be given one for the other in a barter economy tend to be of different value. Their value relation is then abstracted from the given exchange and counted as units of money. Money is, accordingly, an expression of the interdependence of people; it is the most general form of a social relationship.

- Why does Simmel insist that some type of conflict is necessary, rather than agree with those who expect an end to all conflict and a stage of permanent peace?
- Why should equality and liberty be seen as alternatives rather than as political ideals to be implemented at the same time?
- What determines the value of money, according to Simmel?
- Why does Simmel not accept the idea that humans were and are equal by nature?

7

Sociology Saves Lives

Vitalism and the Poor Person

Equality: A Life for the Poor Person?

This book emphasizes what goes on between people as their shared social life. That was pointed out in Chapter 1: Someone wrote these lines and you read them, so this book goes on between reader and writer. Someone talks and somebody else listens, so what is spoken goes on between the two. Money is spent by one person and another person deposits it in the bank, and indeed Simmel's relational interest in money is based on that. It is not this person's unique abilities or that person's characteristic moods Simmel focuses on; rather, it is the special quality of the relationship between two or more persons. In the same way, what he studies about poverty is what goes on between those who do not have enough money and the others around them who *consider them poor*. The topic has been dealt with in the book *Georg Simmel, The Pauper* (Draghici, 2001). The word used by Simmel is *der Arme*.

Sociology was intended by Simmel to be *the study of the quality of relationships*. When interacting with each other, individuals find a way to agree on how to look at what they experience. As is well known, there are as many realities as there are ways of looking at the world: To the nature lover, a forest is a resource of plants and animals; to the logger, it is a chance to cut trees and produce lumber. The nature lover as well as the logger are sure that their point of view is well taken, as long as they communicate in the context of their peers who share their views. And we, the readers of Simmel's writings today, are aware of these limits to human perception: What a person perceives as his or her "reality" is not all there is to say about it. The exciting question is "Under what conditions do we think things are real?" (see Chapter 2).

As we have seen, the lines we read, a book we study, sentences spoken to us, a song we listen to, and even money can be dealt with as existing *between* persons. Obviously, the subject of erotic love falls within Simmel's interest as well, although of course one can research narcissism as a condition describing the love someone feels for himself or herself. Simmel also looks at the law as a quality of a relationship: The way one person treats another person may be legal or illegal (see Chapter 1). Thus, whether the law will be abided by or broken can also be looked at as the quality of a relationship. Indeed, literature, music, art in general, money, love, and law are Simmel's topics precisely because they can be looked at as *qualities of relationships*.

It is in the continuity of this social thought that Simmel turns toward the subject of the poor. He points out that society as a whole can be looked at as consisting of acts performed by individuals carrying out their duties. Everyone participating in the vast societal context has duties to fulfill. But if looked at as action going on inside a relationship, the *duty* of one is at the same time the *right* of another (Simmel, 2009, p. 409). The wealthy church-goer leaving the medieval cathedral after attending the Sunday service may have a *duty* to give alms to the beggar, while the poor person begging may experience the same situation as his *right* to be cared for by a well-to-do fellow Christian.

Simmel's relational approach leads to the plain insight that the right of one becomes the duty of somebody else when the two individuals interact. Just as it is, under certain conditions, the right of the student to be taught, it is the duty of the teacher to teach. And to the right of the teacher to find his students well prepared corresponds the duty of the student to study in advance of the scheduled class. Because the right of one turns out to be the duty of the other, it follows that *right* and *duty* are two aspects of the same performance. This becomes relevant to how Simmel deals with the problem of the poor person: Taking care of the underprivileged is analyzed by him accordingly.

As is typical in Simmel's (2009) reasoning, he tries to voice the opinion of a potential critic or opponent. He expects the representative of a certain school of ethics to contradict his relational idea that interaction in society should be seen as oriented toward rights and duties. Instead, this assumed counterposition would claim, based on a "profound refusal of any inter-individual origin of duty: our duties would be duties toward ourselves, and there would be no others at all" (p. 410). From this point of view, the beggar would have no right to be given anything, but the wealthy man, passing him by, would be inflicted with such guilt that he may be unable to go to sleep the following night. Therefore, if he gives alms, he does it for his own good, not the beggar's. But Simmel does not accept this position.

Next, Simmel (2009) turns to "the different conceptions about providing assistance to the poor" (p. 410). A political system cannot systematically introduce and maintain welfare by depending on the consciences of citizens who are confronted with the hardship of poor persons. Therefore, Simmel returns to his view of the duality of rights and duties. The tradition of a country may allow—or at least tolerate—begging, thereby tacitly defining alms giving as the right of the poor person and at the same time as the duty of members of the general public. But there are different concepts of providing assistance, depending on how the poor person can present his or her claims as a *member of a specific group* of people to which the poor, as well as some better-off people, belong.

If the prevailing view is that the individual is a product of his or her social environment, then it follows that he or she has a right to welfare because poverty is not the fault of the failed person but proof of failure of the group's efforts. But even if more individual responsibility is placed on the citizen, the indisputable fact that there *are* poor persons and that at least some of them cannot be blamed for having become poor must lead to awarding them some right to assistance. This Simmel (2009) sees as necessity because "only when one assumes such a right, at least as a socio-legal fiction, the conduct of poor relief appears to be removed from what is arbitrary, from the dependence on chance financial conditions and other insecurities (p. 410).

A further reason for declaring assistance a *right* of the poor person is to create a psychological condition that makes it possible to *accept* aid without completely losing face; "the dejection, the shame, and the degradation from charity are neutralized for the recipient to the extent that it is not granted out of mercy, a sense of duty, or expediency, but to the extent that it can be demanded" by the needy (Simmel, 2009, p. 410). Simmel places the right to assistance for the poor person side by side with the right to work and the right to one's existence (p. 411). These concepts of human rights have been much under discussion since Simmel's book was first published in 1908.

Relating the right to support in the case of poverty to human rights in general leads Simmel to next look into the foundations of the claims of the poor. From the perspective of sociology, the poor can be defined as members of several social groups. Simmel (2009) provides a list of such possible memberships:

> State, municipal community, parish, professional organization, friendship circles, and families may have as wholes exceedingly different relationships with their membership; still each of these relationships seems to contain an element that is actualized as a right for support in case an individual becomes pauperized. (p. 411)

Simmel explains that the evolutionary origins of such a right for support can be seen in the combination of tribal and religious bonds. They create the sense of closeness that gives rise to the duty to aid a fellow member in need. Also, in developed societies, a religious dimension as foundation of the claims of the poor frequently remains intact.

So far, the reason for giving support to the poor person has been entirely on the side of the receiver; now, Simmel (2009) shifts his attention to the side of the giver. Not only may an individual in need profit from alms giving, but also the person making the donation can be seen as benefitting from the transfer of money or goods. "As Jesus said to the rich young man: give your possession to the poor—obviously his concern was not at all for the poor but rather for the soul of the young man" (p. 412). Alms giving can thus be interpreted as belonging to Christian asceticism: The good works performed by the sinner to enhance the likelihood of achieving salvation. Laudable as that approach may appear, it tends to disrupt the relationship between giver and recipient. The good deeds no longer happen for the sake of the poor person but merely for the sake of the wealthy one because the donations supposedly help him or her go to heaven, or at least make him or her feel good.

Welfare Programs

Making the giver no longer feel responsible for the receiver is potentially dangerous. Masses of excluded individuals subjected to poverty can be seen by governments to be a source of political instability. But the history of revolutions in Europe shows the instigators of drastic political change typically come from the lower middle class and have an intellectual background rather than originating from the ranks of the poor persons. In Germany, Karl Marx received a doctorate in philosophy and in Russia, Lenin held a law degree. The perception, however, is different from these facts: Once a revolution gets under way, the violent armies in support of change are recruited from the lower classes in whose name the better-educated revolutionaries claim to act. Be that as it may, the fear of political instability is a significant motivation for governments to establish a program of social welfare, in order to keep the poor persons on the inside of the social order.

Government programs also support poor persons "in order to make the diminished power of the poor person once again productive for it, and in order to prevent the degeneration of the poor person's descendents" (Simmel, 2009, p. 412). But there is something unique about welfare measures: Simmel points out that in contrast to all other government programs, which are directed at the general public, welfare measures are aimed at a peculiar segment of the population—the poor person—to "relieve individual difficulties" (p. 413). This makes such programs more vulnerable to funding cuts if government spending must be reduced because there will hardly be a broad electoral base in support of the poor.

Simmel moves on to describe and criticize the welfare systems in England and Germany in his days. Too much has changed since to let those statements still be relevant. However, he deals with a problem that has stayed with us: Exercising legal force upon relatives to give money to a family member who has become a pauper. In Germany,

> the high court has decided against an old man in needy circumstances, ruling that he had to provide his only property, a few hundred marks, for the support of an unemployable son, even though he explained credibly that he would soon himself be unemployable and that the money was his only reserve. It is extremely doubtful whether one can still speak in this case of a moral right of the son. (Simmel, 2009, p. 416)

The legal reasoning was to protect the general public from excessive burdens and accordingly make the family responsible for taking care of its poor, so the person in need could survive without government interference. Simmel points to the problem without commenting on it.

Poverty requires welfare programs because it is potentially life threatening. If the quality of being a poor person is ascribed to someone, his or her life is seen to be limited. Our lives occur within the limitations we experience in time, space, opportunities, and other facts that set borders to what we expect to determine the scope of our activities. But as we become aware of them, put them into perspective, and think of ways to overcome them, we also limit their significance. All human beings live under the severe duty of becoming what they are destined to be. They can, however, only realize their potential if they see their limits, yet then not stop at those in resignation, but rather transcend them, go beyond them. This is essentially the background for Simmel's "vitalism," and it can be seen as the foundation for his entire philosophical and sociological thinking and specifically for his theory of change.

Vitalism and the Sociological Impact of Life

In order to describe change and to identify the forces that propel it, Simmel looks for energies inherent in the lives of persons. He writes that *life* as it manifests itself in such drives as love, religiosity, admiration of aesthetic beauty, or in other types of creativity, cannot evolve in society unless protected by the forms those drives are equipped with, such as marriage to give love a form, church to give religiosity a form, art to give the drive toward aesthetic beauty a form. On the one hand, these forms protect life as it manifests itself in drives, but on the other hand, if forms lose the ability to adjust to the dynamics of life, they may become oppressive and develop into a threat to life itself due to alienation. Thus to Simmel, life with the drives it produces provides the contents of culture, while structured interaction supplies a form to protect its existence.

Simmel takes this confrontation in life between content, the creativity it produces, and form, the protection (or the alienated and petrified inhibition) of creativity, as a point of departure for a critical stance toward society: A given society as it exists, or existed in history, is not necessarily good simply because it is there. He carefully develops the criteria for good or bad by inspecting the relation between *content* and *form*. He does that on the basis of an evolutionary approach to the developing human condition. He assumes, as it were, that societies as well as individuals are step by step moving forward toward a better way of life, one that may not have existed before. Any *form* getting in the way of that development should be criticized.

In his numerous publications, Simmel presents many applications of his optimistic and evolutionary approach toward life, as follows:

1. Life and conflict: Life, with its innate tendency to produce conflict between individuals as content, depends upon forms to channel that dangerously aggressive drive. To illustrate, Simmel (1903b, pp. 1013, 1018) mentions dueling in traditional societies and competition in modern ones. Consequently, he sees an evolution from the old fashioned form of a duel, in the course of which a person was usually killed, to the more contemporary form of dueling, competition, which, as we have seen, he describes as a resolution of conflict resulting in benefits for everybody.

2. Life and worldviews: Life produces the will to believe (William James) among human beings as content. From the distant past to the present, societies developed more and more complex belief systems as interpretations of physical and social reality, from theories for handling the daily routine all the way up to philosophical and religious ideas. The latter are forms the will to believe will take under certain social conditions, forms such as a creed, a set of dogmas, or classical texts that make self-confident behavior possible for the believer. Only large groups can provide such orientation, based on the consensus of large numbers of persons; the isolated individual cannot. This points to the ambivalence of individualization: In step with freeing the person from collective pressure, it will also lead to more experience of insecurity. In order to study that ambivalence in more detail, Simmel looks at some of the works of Spinoza, Rousseau, Kant, Fichte, Marx, Schopenhauer, Nietzsche, Bergson, and others.

3. Life and art: Simmel thinks that in life there is an innate admiration for what appears to be beautiful. He identifies it as something like an aesthetic drive, which—as was stated above—as content would compare to love, religiosity, or a general curiosity. The concomitant form, or structured interaction, of love might be marriage; of religiosity it is a church or a sect; of curiosity it can be scholarship and a college; and of the aesthetic drive it is art and an art museum. Simmel also sees a close connection between the search for beauty and love because both are often nurtured by the aesthetic drive. A lover typically experiences his or her partner as particularly beautiful, sometimes to the amazement of her contemporaries who are not in love with that person.

At the end of Chapter 4, we saw that to Simmel, religiosity is contained in life itself. But life cannot be a form; it requires forming to be lived. Life thus operates within the human individual as an independent force. What Simmel has in mind is not, however, in any way close to fate or a notion of an individual calling. He uses those concepts in different contexts. His notion of life is connected to his evolutionary theory, and it is the collective life of humankind as a species that is reflected in the individual experiences of the person. In order to make that idea more plausible, he looks for illustrations from everyday occurrences: What we feel to be our needs and intuitive desires frequently are derived from images that originate in comfortable religious or other ethical customs and traditions (Simmel, 1893, p. 394). As soon as we reflect on those, we will grudgingly recognize them as dated prejudices, and we still will have the most difficult time of getting rid of them because they have their origin in the collective life of the past.

In order better to understand problems of cultural change and moderniza-tion, Simmel suggests considering the dualism or confrontation between two worldviews: a current one that is in opposition to a worldview of the past. Normally we are not aware of this conflict because what has been handed down to us from the distant past via whichever channel has been relegated to our subconscious emotional reserves, and we normally do not even have access to those. The second section of Chapter 3, Toward an Ethics of Indi-vidualization, addresses in part the problem of relieving the person from those restraints of the collective past. At the same time, that section reports Simmel's resistance to Kant's belief in a rational foundation for ethics. If we want to be realistic, Simmel thinks, we should not expect *reason* but *collective emotions* to guide the evolution of cultured life.

And it is precisely this evolution of cultured life that raises Simmel's con-cern: In order to be happy, humans must be able to experience the realization of their goals. Those goals, however, change from concrete fulfillment as ends (like purchasing a comfortable home) to acquiring the means (like studying harder to make more money). Thus the collective images of happy lives are moved further and further out of reach of the individual and are finally even relegated to an area beyond our consciousness (Simmel, 1892, p. 89). Those images are thus driven by emotions. That happens also because more and more irrational material and legal requirements are introduced that must be met before fulfillment can be expected. According to Simmel's fears, that causes the modern individual increasingly to concentrate his or her life on the acquisition of *means* (like money), regardless of the ethical desirability of *goals* the fulfillment of which the means make possible.

As a result, the living conditions of modern humans will become more and more complex. The struggle for existence will turn into a struggle for the means needed to exist. The interests motivating people to act in a given way will not be geared toward directly achieving or avoiding happiness and pain, but instead toward finding ways and means as steps forward on the approach. The downside of all that is, to Simmel (1892), that there will be such an enormous multitude of tools required that people will lose sight of why they wanted to realize their goals in the first place (p. 89).

What can be done about these trends? Keeping the poor person alive, keeping him or her from starvation as well as rescuing the average contem-porary from desperation can possibly be achieved following the same path. Simmel recommends an intellectual endeavor of distancing *interests* from *persons*. Frequently, when asked about an obvious defect in human interac-tion, the person questioned will reply with, "It is not my fault." The person wanting information may insist, "I am not interested in whose fault this is; I just want to find out how it happened." Or, to add the illustration given by

Simmel himself, to the real scholar it makes no difference whether he or she makes the discovery or some other person makes it, as long as a groundbreaking new insight can be obtained in research (Simmel, 1892, p. 152). In both cases, the bias of the illustration is in favor of increasing the distance from the person.

Detaching the interest in an achievement from the interest in the person is, according to Simmel, one of the most important processes in the evolution of culture. This process can start with an egotistic motivation or with an altruistic one, but while it unfolds it leaves the person-oriented drives more and more behind and finally gets its impetus purely from devotion to the subject matter (Simmel, 1892, p. 152). This attitude of "I do not care whose fault it is, but I want it to be fixed!" has the consequence of making the notion of revenge an impossible point of view. Simmel quotes Plato, for whom there can be no personal justification for any deed that is objectively evil. And *that* leads to the unconditional prohibition of revenge (p. 154).

Simmel thinks Plato was the first philosopher who presented the idea that something may be good or bad regardless of the person attached to it. This independent goodness would then become a quality of our action if we follow the ideal; it would give our conduct a suprapersonal goal. Later philosophers have seen the goal in the realization of universal reason or of the kingdom of God. The frightening reversal of progress, which had been increasing the distance from the *person* in favor of serving a *principle,* can be seen in political movements that demand allegiance not to a constitution or an established democratic order but instead to a dictator of rightist or leftist persuasion. The catastrophes of the last century have been futile attempts at re-personalizing ethical orientation by forcing individuals to follow "leaders" rather than ideals.

On the other hand, the ambivalence of the human condition entails the experience that detaching the interest in a subject matter from the interest in the person affected by it can become a nightmare, if carried to extremes. We can often observe this in contemporary bureaucracy. Admittedly, the interest in the person is an *impediment* to gaining insights and orientations: Ideals, as guiding principles, are much preferable in scholarship and ethics. However, at the other end, so to speak, where insights are applied in day-to-day conduct, interest in the person is *needed* for any cultured interaction. The government bureaucrat often uses his obligation to serve abstract principles as an excuse for treating his clients as if they were impersonal entities rather than human beings. This is particularly painful if the client is a poor person applying for welfare.

As in the case of this dilemma of devotion to a person on the one hand and following abstract principles on the other, Simmel (1918, p. 1) sees life as flowing along constantly between two limitations. We assume a limit above and a limit below in order to get a sense of the space available to us. Humans need borders in order to find themselves, and they also need to go beyond those borders once they have recognized them. Until we leave the town we grew up in, we do not know it is a small town. First we profit from accepting a limitation, then we accept it by going beyond it and looking at it from the outside (p. 3).

Individuals can only realize their potential if they see their limits but transcend them. Typical limits the person finds himself or herself confronted with are emotional biases. Unrecognized and not admitted, those would be most difficult to overcome. In 1892, Simmel introduced the concept of suppressed consciousness (prior to Freud's 1895–1896 publications). He contrasted two worldviews: the current one and a worldview of the past that is in opposition to it. Typically, the latter cannot be overcome because it eludes intellectual critique. Simmel helps his readers to recognize those limitations and thereby to deal with them in leading a less prejudiced life.

Unlike Freud, Simmel does not focus on the individual; his primary goal is social life. He warns that we should not expect reason but collective emotions to guide the evolution of cultured life. Emotions, however, are personal, and as a remedy against widespread irrational collective behavior, Simmel recommends distancing the interests from the person. As we find ourselves recipients of government services, frequently the bureaucratic style of impersonal interaction is an unpleasant and unfounded misinterpretation of the need to distance the interests from the person. Thus, bringing the person back in can be the result of acknowledging this limitation to life. We must state, in fairness, that there are many government offices in which this goal is realized.

We have seen a few of the limitations that give life direction: An action performed in a social context may be motivated by a sense of duty, but at the same time it may respect the right of somebody else. Rights and duties limit people's lives yet give them an opportunity to act beyond what they owe or are entitled to get. In the history of alms giving, the rights/duty limitation is dissolved at one point, and the wealthy performs a good deed for his or her own religious benefit. That disrupts the relationship between giver and recipient, potentially makes large numbers of poor persons politically dangerous, and thus motivates governments to engage in social welfare. Limitations disrupting the bond between the alms giver and the poor person cause it to go beyond the one on one relationship and help transform it into a political program.

Finally, on the highest level of abstraction, Simmel discusses the limitations in life set by the way goals and means are related. In modern times, it becomes more and more difficult to keep the primary hopes geared to the pursuit of happiness in sight. Instead, there will be such a multitude of tools required to achieve one's goals that people may lose sight of why they wanted them in the first place.

Conclusion

In Chapter 7, Simmel's ideas about the poor person and about life are combined. Being poor is looked at as the quality of a relationship. Taking care of poor persons is placed in the context of the duality of rights and duties: The same action, like supporting a poor person, can be seen as the right of one and the duty of another. Because large groups of dissatisfied poor persons are perceived as potential hotbeds of political unrest, governments develop welfare programs. The considered purpose of those is to keep the poor person inside society.

Simmel sees life in the context of his evolutionary theory. The life of humankind as it has unfolded over millennia is reflected in the lives of individuals. To predict the path culture and society will take in the future, it is not realistic to rely on human reason alone. Collective emotions will play a significant part in evolution. Simmel recommends distancing interests from persons. In addition, in the foreseeable future, it may become difficult to keep primary hopes in sight. Instead, there will be such a multitude of tools required to achieve one's goals that people may lose sight of a meaningful purpose for those goals.

Here are some questions for discussion:

- What does it take, from Simmel's point of view, to become a "poor person"?
- What are the consequences if the person receiving support feels he or she is entitled to help?
- There are several reasons why most governments design some type of welfare program. What are some of them?
- How does Simmel see "tools" flourish like weeds in a garden and outgrow the goals the fulfillment of which they were originally meant to serve?

8

Further Readings

Living in Big Cities

This final chapter is written with the assumption that the reader will have read Simmel's "The Metropolis and Mental Life" (1950) or will read it parallel to inspecting the following paragraphs. Generations of American sociology students have been using the textbook by Kurt Wolff (Trans.), *The Sociology of Georg Simmel*. Deena Weinstein, together with her husband, the philosopher M. A. Weinstein, has contributed significantly toward making the work of Simmel known in the English-speaking world of scholarship. She has selected from the Wolff book the article "The Metropolis and Mental Life," which Simmel presented as a lecture in 1903. Weinstein (n.d.) adapted it for student use and provided footnotes to explain what Simmel had in mind.

The reason this particular text is reread here is its wide scope and its compelling argument. In a way, it summarizes Simmel's social thought. He typically describes life in the big cities as ambivalent; it obviously brings about progress, but at the same time it also endangers the autonomy of the individual. This happens because of technological innovations as well as the transition to a new stage in the development of culture. Simmel thinks in terms of evolution, as we have seen in the previous chapters. He interprets the fate of humankind as a fight with nature for our bodily existence. This fight undergoes multiple transformations in the cause of history: Adapting to life in the big city means entering upon the adventure of its latest transformation.

In the continuity of Western civilization this did not occur suddenly, of course. Simmel looks at recent centuries and compares what happened culturally in the 18th century to what happened in the 19th century. The former resulted in shedding traditional bonds imposed upon the individual by government and church. Those restrictions hampered innovations in ethics and in the economy. As a reaction against that rigidity, liberal ideas were justified by the notion that the human being was benign by nature and was therefore entrusted with his or her own development. The image of humans that resulted was perhaps close to the way Tarzan has been portrayed in America. To this then-new idea of freedom, the 19th century added functional specialization of work as an opportunity for the person to become irreplaceable. This concept referred to an ever-increasing division of labor, making it harder to replace one person with another.

Faced with a growing interdependence between individuals, each person also experienced having more power over the other, or concomitantly, feeling threatened by the influence of the other. In line with this, Nietzsche expected the most ruthless struggle among individuals. Socialism reacted by demanding the suppression of all competition, as we mentioned in Chapter 6. Simmel sees the same general trend behind both positions: the struggle of the individual against being leveled down and made irrelevant by the innovations big cities bring to modern life. This struggle can lead to ruthless selfishness as well as to socialist ideas (and, indeed, to a combination of both). The basic problem, then, is the confrontation between the desire of the individual to protect his or her autonomy and the various pressures to adjust to external forces in modern big cities.

This tension was Simmel's topic in the remainder of the lecture. Kurt Wolff decided to translate Simmel's title as "metropolis" rather than "big city." A German by origin, Wolff knew that Simmel referred to the capital, Berlin, where he experienced what he was talking about. Berlin is a big city as well as the German capital, which makes it Germany's only metropolis. However, in applying Simmel's insight to a wider and more cosmopolitan reality, it may be just as appropriate to translate *Die Großstädte und das Geistesleben* literally as *The Big Cities and Their Culture,* particularly because Simmel's original title uses the plural, which is lost if rendered as *The Metropolis.*

Weinstein (n.d.) numbers the sections of the text to make reading it seem less discouraging. In her adaptation, this is the beginning of Section 2. It starts with Simmel's observation that living in big cities gets on people's nerves. Too many impulses reach the person at the same time—noises, colors, persons, objects—regardless of whether or not they respond to an interest of the individual, they impose themselves on him or her indiscriminately. This results in an overstimulation that threatens the ability of the city dweller to concentrate on the items relevant to him or her. This is particularly threatening if the person has been used to living in a small town because there the style of life is vastly different from life in the big city.

Simmel describes rural life and life in a small town as similar. Although obviously there is a difference between the two, the characteristic threats to the autonomy of the individual are absent in both cases. The threats are peculiar to city life. A higher level of consciousness is required in the big city. This starts with crossing a busy street, where any lack of attention could be life threatening and would certainly be fatal in heavy traffic. In the country and the small town, on the other hand, "the rhythm of life and sensory mental imagery flows more slowly, more habitually, and more evenly" (Weinstein, n.d.).

That is why living in the big city is more stressful by comparison, and that is why people who have adjusted to it tend to appear more sophisticated. City life demands a high level of attention and rationality; country life is based more distinctly on emotional relationships. Accordingly, the city person will react with his or her head rather than with the heart. Living in the big city is bearable and successful only on the condition that the intellect is cultured and developed as a counterbalance over against too-frequent and too-obvious emotional outbursts in interaction.

Section 3 starts by reminding the reader that the economy is an impressive illustration for the needed prevalence of the intellect over the emotions. Decisions must be calculated in units of money to anticipate their effect. Formal rules must be followed regardless what the personal lot of the participant may be, and implementing them often implies harshness and a built-in lack of consideration because that is required to keep the system functioning. The uniqueness and individuality of the person will have to be disregarded, and that, indeed, is how the sophisticated person typically reacts to the individuality of others. The money economy must center its attention on what is common to all.

Simmel sees the big city as the principal location of the modern money economy. Emotions like love or hatred are linked to real or imagined qualities of individuals. Where individuality is suppressed, emotions lose ground, unless they are resurrected as political or religious mass movements. The sober rational relations required in economic interaction lead to giving human beings numbers. In Simmel's day, there still was a sense of the absurdity of giving a number to a person. Numbering individuals demonstrates that unique personal traits do not matter. The money economy leads to reducing individuality to quantity, expressed in the simple question, How much? The rule to abstain from showing emotions in public, the disinterest in personal uniqueness, and the tendency to reckon with quantities rather than qualities are integrated into an urban lifestyle that treats customers, employees, and even acquaintances with distance and aloofness.

Simmel points out that this applies to conditions of the modern economy in general. In a less-developed society, commercial goods were produced to order for a customer the producer knew personally. As long as the relations between partners in economic exchange were interactions among acquaintances, the conditions that prevailed were like those of the countryside and the small town. The modern big city, however, houses producers who do not make things for people they know; they supply their goods to an anonymous market. Because one partner no longer knows the other, their interaction is totally devoid of any emotion like kindness or being considerate. Doing business via a market means that only rational calculation counts, based on the anonymity of the partners. It also means that the small-group behavior of personal relationships has become dysfunctional in the big city, even though the typical well-trained salesperson will give the impression that it still matters.

Weinstein (n.d.) starts the fourth section with Simmel's surprising equation between the money economy and the natural sciences. What they have in common is the preference for quantities rather than qualities, combined with the will to perform calculations. To transform the world into an arithmetic problem is the frightening goal shared by the natural sciences and the modern money economy. This inclination extends to the hope to find a mathematical formula for what goes on in the world in general and in society in particular (see Chapter 2).

It is, moreover, based on the need for precision. Whereas in the countryside and the small town people may have told time by the chimes of the church bell, the big city person without a watch is unthinkable. Everyone needs access to the exact time by whatever technical means in order to be punctual for his or her appointments. The rationality of economic exchanges as well as of the big city culture that enables it require absolute reliability and punctuality with merciless strictness, for otherwise the complicated system of interaction in the big city would collapse in total chaos.

What does all this mean for the personalities of city dwellers? Simmel admits that in spite of the leveling effects, autonomous and independent characters with strong personalities are participants in cultured urban life. However, he claims, they are the exception rather than the rule. Big city normalcy would be represented by those who have subjected their ways to the commanding traits: intellectuality, punctuality, calculability, precision, and reliability. These demands upon the modern person would necessarily lead to being, as David Riesman (1950/2001) has called it, other-directed.

Riesman (1950/2001) compares the other-directed individual to someone with a built-in radar, constantly picking up guiding signals from the social environment. The strong personality, by contrast, is like a human being with a compass giving him or her a direction that is above debate. The intuitive personality from country and small town listens to emotional impulses from within; the person well adjusted to big city life and the money economy is largely directed from without. Under these conditions, modernity will make it harder and harder for creative nonconformists to evolve in opposition to the established system of interaction.

Weinstein's (n.d.) Section 5 starts with Simmel's statement that due to the ambivalence of many phenomena in culture and society, the modern urban tendencies have not only had a leveling effect but also resulted in promoting a highly personal subjectivity inside big cities. This brings him to introducing and discussing the so-called blasé attitude. In a footnote, Weinstein defines that as "unresponsiveness to stimulation; refusal or inability to be emotionally moved by or involved in people and things." Being blasé is frequently a reaction in self-defense against an unbearable multitude of sensual impressions. This reaction comes with attitudes such as "I have seen this before" or "this is nothing new to me." Although we usually consider it unfriendly, or at least unattractive, for a person to expose a blasé mood, Simmel describes it as a result of metropolitan intellectuality and adds that uncultured persons will not be blasé.

The money economy gives the blasé attitude an additional dimension because all things can be purchased for money and thus lose their specific qualities. The question "what is special and perhaps unique about this object?" is replaced by the question "how much does it cost?" Thus, as money becomes the common denominator, it encourages the distant aloofness displayed by the blasé person. Eventually it may contribute to a sense of worthlessness experienced by those persons themselves.

This is explained in detail in Section 6. The following part of the text expands on the idea that city life is too stressful and too demanding for the nerves of an open-minded person, and to protect him or her from nervous breakdowns, some defensive measures are in order. In addition to being blasé, the city dweller will resort to formality in social contacts. This will make it superfluous to get emotionally involved. It will, instead, give superficial interactions a degree of legitimacy.

The danger Simmel sees appear on the horizon of city culture is an all-out indifference as well as excessive openness to the other. Both extremes must be avoided. Toward that goal, he even justifies a degree of antipathy in big-city interaction. This antipathy should be latent to keep it from being converted into open antagonism. It protects the person by keeping him or her at a distance from random others. Without such mechanisms of distancing it would not be possible to lead a healthy and successful city life. Section 8 describes how these techniques of keeping one's mental health under urban conditions result in an unusual amount of personal freedom.

Next Simmel elaborates on his theory of social evolution, starting with the small circle of highly coherent social relations. This was explained here in Chapter 3, using the example of the Quakers. The small circles provide security at the expense of freedom. In Section 9, Simmel points out that the ancient *polis*, commonly admired by contemporary man as, for instance, democratic Athens, forced their inhabitants to conduct what Simmel calls small-town interaction. From the perspective of history, the modern culture of the big city is a recent and most remarkable achievement in personal freedom. This must be seen clearly in spite of all the various dangers and impediments that have been described here about urban culture.

In ancient Athens, Simmel sees a confrontation between highly individualized personalities and constant small-town pressure toward conformity. As a result, weaker persons were suppressed while stronger ones were provoked to develop their unique individuality. To this Simmel adds his conviction that the most general, most far reaching, or as we would perhaps say today, the most global-minded contributions to life are closely related to the most individual ones. Confronted with petty small-town provincialism, the individual feels hemmed in. Turned loose inside the big city and surrounded by anonymous masses, the bodily proximity may result in two opposite consequences: It may cause him or her to become fully conscious of how utterly free city life makes the person, or conversely, it has the potential of arousing the feeling of extreme loneliness while getting lost in the crowds.

Section 10 continues to apply Simmel's theory of social evolution, according to which the social circles giving the person his or her identity gradually become wider and wider. The wider the circle, the more freedom is awarded the individual. The big city is not only itself a social reality of wider company; in addition, Simmel sees it as the seat of cosmopolitanism. Cosmopolitanism is

> the attitude that nothing human is foreign to me; that the whole realm of culture, wherever it originates, is open to me—I draw no boundaries around parts of culture that make those parts belong only to separate groups (e.g., "Italian culture is only for Italians"). (Weinstein, n.d.)

To the extent that this conviction is fostered in a big city, its culture is global, referring to humankind in general as a worldwide community. The big city fulfills functions making it extend beyond its physical boundaries.

The eleventh section of this text refers again to the high degree of division of labor in the big city. This leads Simmel to the topic of competition, which we discussed at the beginning of Chapter 6. Competition for job opportunities and for financial gain induces people to specialize more and more in order to increase their chances of success. "This process promotes differentiation, refinement, and the enrichment of the public's needs, which obviously must lead to growing personal differences within this public" (Weinstein, n.d.). This observation is carried over into Section 12. Competition not only causes people to specialize in their vocational abilities, but to want to be different and hope to appear unique. This is attempted by wearing clothing according to the latest fashion (cf. Chapter 3).

In Section 12, Simmel pays attention to qualitative differences between human contacts in the big city as compared to the small town. In the latter environment, people generally have more time available to them, or in any case, it is considered polite at least to appear to have time for the other person. In the big city situation, by contrast, it is fashionable to be busy and short of time. Contacts tend to be short and far apart by comparison. This necessitates a concentration on the moment and makes the city dweller try to impress his counterpart quickly by his or her appearance and by a few poignant remarks because there is no time for a drawn-out conversation. The whole point is to be remembered as special.

The thirteenth section of the text confronts objective culture with subjective culture. Objective culture as it manifests itself in documented texts, in available works of art, and in other manifestations of human creativity over the millennia grows further and further. The cultured individual who in his or her education attempts to keep track of all there is to know and, in the case of the fine arts, to practice falls behind in a discouraging fashion. This is, to Simmel, not only a plausible consequence of the multitude of details in objective culture: It is in addition to the decreasing accomplishments of the individual person. It would be simplifying matters to attribute that to weaknesses of the education institutions alone. What contributes to this deplorable trend is a side effect of the division of labor. It forces the individual to become increasingly one-sided in the course of his or her specialization. That, in turn, makes him or her less likely to be able to cope with the vastness of objective culture.

Finally, in the last and fourteenth section of the text, Simmel writes about two types of individualism in big cities: individual independence and encouragement of individuality. The first can be associated with political ambitions aimed at giving the unique person more opportunity to develop in spite of the undue pressures toward obedience and conformity. The second follows from a successful implementation of the first: Individuals are now allowed and encouraged to distinguish themselves from each other. The value orientation shifts from representing humanity in general to realizing the person's unique potential. According to Simmel, history takes its course along the dynamic development that entails these two forms of individuality in modern society.

I end by quoting Simmel's last paragraph of—as I would prefer to title it—*The Big Cities and Their Culture*, in the translation of Kurt Wolff:

> For the metropolis presents the peculiar conditions which are revealed to us as the opportunities and the stimuli for the development of both these ways of allocating roles to men. Therewith these conditions gain a unique place, pregnant with inestimable meanings for the development of psychic existence. The metropolis reveals itself as one of those great historical formations in which opposing streams which enclose life unfold, as well as join one another with equal right. However, in this process the currents of life, whether their individual phenomena touch us sympathetically or antipathetically, entirely transcend the sphere for which the judge's attitude is appropriate. Since such forces of life have grown into the roots and into the crown of the whole of the historical life in which we, in our fleeting existence, as a cell, belong only as a part, it is not our task either to accuse or to pardon, but only to understand. (Weinstein, n.d.)

We owe this English-language text to Kurt Wolf and Deena Weinstein. Simmel's publications have been selectively translated into English by such prominent American scholars as Guy Oakes (Simmel, 1977, 1980), Tamotsu Shibutani (1955), and Anselm Strauss (1959). The latter two have shown that the approach taken by Simmel does not limit the scope of his work to small-group research or formal sociology. In their well-known book *The Social Construction of Reality*, Peter L. Berger and Thomas Luckmann (1966) refer to Simmel six times. In Erving Goffman's *Frame Analysis* (1974), the reader finds an application and convincing continuation of Simmel ideas: Simmel's *form* becomes Goffman's *frame*. Neil J. Smelser (1995), in his *Problematics of Sociology*, summarized Simmel's achievements convincingly.

The most current translations have been used in this book: Chapter 4 is based on the 1997 English-language edition of Simmel's *Essays on Religion*. The sections of Chapter 5 on the demise of the patriarchal household and on marriage as a special dyad rely on the 2009 translation of Simmel's 1908 book *Soziologie*. The subtitle of the 2009 translation is *Inquiries Into the Construction of Social Forms*. The German original was available in 2008 in two versions: (1) the sixth edition by Duncker and Humblot in Berlin, the publisher who has the original copyright to much of Simmel's works; and

(2) Volume 11 in the collected works of Georg Simmel (*Gesamtausgabe in 24 Bänden*) available from Suhrkamp publishers in Frankfurt. The Suhrkamp cloth edition is sold out, but the paperback version can be ordered.

Thomas M. Kemple (2007) has recently been the most active author in commenting on and translating Simmel. Together with Ulrich Teucher, he published translations of Simmel's largely unknown texts "Rome" (1898), "Florence" (1906), "Venice" (1907), "The Social Boundary" (1908), "The Metaphysics of Death" (1910), "The Problem of Fate" (1913), "Goethe and Youth" (1914), and "Become What You Are" (1915) in a special issue of *Theory, Culture & Society*. In an interesting comparison of Max Weber and W. E. B. Du Bois with Simmel, Kemple (2009) looked at their takes on certain aspects of music. When one of the leading scholars in Simmel research, David Frisby (1944–2010) died, Kemple (2010) devoted a special issue of *Theory, Culture & Society* to Frisby's memory.

Finally, in 2012, Austin Harrington and Thomas M. Kemple edited a special issue of that journal on "Simmel's Sociological Metaphysics." In that issue, the editors make available the English translation of selections from Simmel's writings for the journal *Jugend:* "Beyond Beauty" (anecdote, 1897); "Only a Bridge" (poem, 1901); "Money Alone Doesn't Bring Happiness" (snapshot *sub specie aeternitatis,* 1901); "The Maker of Lies" (snapshot, 1901); "Relativity" (snapshot, 1902); and "La Duse" (snapshot, 1901). Simmel predicted the enormous changes in culture and social politics that occurred during the 20th century. The methodological impetus that sociology owes to Simmel lives on in a new way of thinking. That is precisely what Simmel wanted sociology to be: A new way of looking at old phenomena, approaching what appeared to have become familiar from a novel perspective and thus generating fresh insights.

Conclusion

This text on Georg Simmel's social thought presents sociology in the context of the liberal arts. Society is a central topic. It consists of a sum of interactions. In the course of such interactions reality is socially constructed. Influences impacting the construction process include emotions. They not only codetermine what we do, but even what we perceive as real. Simmel does not want to see the sciences become the sole source of orientation. Society is possible for three reasons: (1) individuals are generalized into categories of people, (2) a person's integration into society always leaves out some aspects due to the uniqueness of him or her, and (3) the collectivity demands that each member is different so he or she can find his or her special place in society compatible with his or her individuality.

Simmel deals with the structure of society and with instructions directed to persons how to conduct themselves. The latter are usually referred to as *social norms*. Simmel sees change on both levels of analysis: The structure opens up, allowing us to live in wider company; the norms adjust to this evolution by admitting ideas for a dynamic ethics. These changes are the requirements to be met in order to enable individualization as the decisive trait of modernization.

Simmel points out that it takes courage for the individual to be different to the point of becoming a stranger and thereby potentially an innovator. Individuals may be reluctant to live the lives of innovators for two reasons: (1) fear of losing the approval of friends and other persons close to them, and (2) fear of loss of identity. Many of the great innovators had to endure persecution and exile. They are remembered today for their courage as well as their contribution to cultural evolution.

The sociology of religion needs a definition of religion suitable for this particular academic field of research: Religion is a system of beliefs that defines life after death as real. In addition, it must be based on personal relationships with one or several immortal persons that are believed to be eternal. Simmel suggests that the established religions leave their respective transcendental worlds of ideas and observe the unique impulses of life itself in order to regain relevance.

In his reflections on the family, he describes the mother-child dyad as the center. Biological fatherhood is seen by him as a late development in the evolution of culture. Simmel explains changes following his rule of reversal: At first marriage arrangements made by family members precede romantic love, then that is reversed. Simmel also looks at the division of labor between genders, first on the individual level between one woman and one man, then on the group level between all women and all men of one society confronting each other, and finally on the division of labor within the group of women: Some women become academics; others are left behind. Finally, he explains why the demise of the patriarchal household is unavoidable. Then he describes the uniqueness of marriage in comparison to all the other dyads.

This text also deals with competition and with money. Conflict is necessary to promote evolution, and competition is desirable because it is an indirect way of fighting and because it occurs to the benefit of other people. Money is, to Simmel, the most powerful illustration for the social construction of reality. Its value is ascribed to it, but due to alienation, that definition process is not acknowledged. The value of money originates in exchange situations. Being poor is looked at as the quality of a relationship.

Simmel sees life in the context of his evolutionary theory. The life of humankind as it has unfolded over millennia is reflected in the lives of individuals. To predict the path culture and society will take in the future, it is not realistic to rely on human reason alone. Collective emotions will play a significant part in evolution. The text ends with re-reading Simmel's well-known lecture on mental life in the metropolis about the impact living in a big city has on cultural change.

The volume ends with these questions:

- Can Simmel's social thought give orientation at the present time to take a creative and critical stance toward contemporary society? How can that be achieved?
- How can Simmel's approach be used today to help sociology become convincing as well as useful?
- What may be the reasons why so many sociologists are indebted to Simmel, yet little reference to his work is made by others?
- Why is Simmel's social thought more influential in sociological research related to culture (religion, art, ethics) than in other areas of sociology?

Glossary

Alienation (1) Due to alienation, something loses its original beneficial purpose and starts leading a dubious life of its own. (2) In the theory of Karl Marx: A person produces a good but is then not considered the owner of it. (3) In the context of ancient Roman law: Conferring property rights from one owner to another owner.

Ancient Greek philosophy Can be divided between (a) the pre-Socratic philosophers (Thales, Pythagoras, Parmenides, Heraclitus) and (b) Socrates, Plato and Aristotle. It extended in time between about 600 and 300 BCE. It raised the question of being (Do we just dream of it or does it really exist?) and developed the concept of nature as a self-ordering system (Thales).

Comte, Auguste (1798–1857) French philosopher who invented the term *sociology.*

Content To Simmel, any one of those driving forces that move individual persons to interact with others. Examples he mentions are impulses, interests, inclinations, and psychological conditions of a person that cause humans to turn toward one another. Other illustrations of content are hunger, love, and religiosity (See also **Form**).

Cultural evolution A theory describing how a culture evolves over time, applied to phenomena such as language, religious creeds, forms of music, poetry, and social and political organizations (See also **Evolutionary theory**).

Dilthey, Wilhelm (1833–1911) German philosopher.

Dynamic ethics Rules for behavior that change over time.

Emotions Strong drives from within the person determining the process of cognition (What do I want to know?) and the course of action taken (What do I want to do?).

Equality   Individuals seen as (a) equipped with identical qualities, so one of them can replace the other, or (b) related to the same value context (as fellow countrymen or children of God), so each must be regarded as equally valuable.

Evolutionary theory   Biological theory that explains the process of physical change in plants and animals over time (See also **Cultural evolution**).

Exclusivity   A system of ethics that stresses the superiority of a certain group of people over all others (See also **Universalism**).

Family types   Distinguished by determining (a) who is in charge of the clan: matriarchal (rule of the mother) or patriarchal (rule of the father); or (b) from whom do my relatives and I descend: matrilineal (from a common mother), patrilineal (from a common father), or bilateral (from common parents).

Form   The mode of interaction among individuals by which content (e.g., love, religiosity, or admiration of aesthetic beauty) achieves social reality (e.g., marriage gives love a form, a church gives religiosity a form, art gives the drive toward aesthetic beauty a form; see also **Content**).

Humanities   The study of the history and philosophy of the human condition.

Individualization   As the decisive trait of modernization, individualization requires recognizing and developing to the fullest the innate potential of each person. Fulfillment of this task hinges on the courage of the individual to be different from others and to deviate from expectations imposed on him or her, to the point of becoming a stranger.

Interpretive sociology   Also called *Verstehen* or humanistic sociology. From the perspective of this approach, the objects of knowledge are the mental operations of acting persons (i.e., the cognitive and emotional procedures within human beings whose behavior is being studied). It is these cognitive and emotional procedures that the researcher attempts to reconstruct. Whether or not he can successfully accomplish this can only be determined if interpretation (*Verstehen)* is possible (i.e., if the sociologist can successfully take the attitude of the other).

Modernization   (a) The liberation from the narrow, village-type order of social relationships that provide security because of their limited number, or (b) the basis for initiating contacts with human beings who live far away and in different cultural contexts, with the tendency toward a cosmopolitan or global orientation.

Physics of the social   An earlier name for sociology.

Poor person   A person not seen as someone belonging to a statistical category with a certain below-level income, but as someone who is *dealt with by others as being poor* (labeling).

Pragmatism   The philosophy of action. Action, as Socrates requires, is to be guided by rational knowledge. In ancient Greek, this applies in the moral and political sphere in the same way as in the sphere of craftsmanship and technology. Simmel derives his principles of pragmatism from Plato's Socrates.

Processual thinking   A mental orientation describing how a culture evolves over time (See also **Cultural evolution**).

Qualities of relationships   The primary reality is what goes on between people. It is not *this* person's unique abilities or *that* person's characteristic moods; rather it is the special quality of the relationship between two or more persons. Sociology is *the study of the qualities of relationships* as fundamental social realities.

Secret   An indispensible means for distinguishing between people who are close and others who are kept at a distance. The person closest to us knows everything about us because we tell them everything. The greater the distance, the more we withhold knowledge from others, because the respective information is "none of their business." Accordingly, we distinguish by distance and are unable and unwilling to treat all our contacts equally with regard to supplying information.

Social construction of reality   Society consists of a sum of interactions. In the course of such interactions, reality is socially constructed. It follows from this construction process that competing views of reality result and that there are alternative perspectives from which social reality can be looked at.

Social movements   Collective action taken by the masses and classes motivated by political, religious, or other value orientation with the goal to initiate political change.

Social structure   The forms ascribed to inequality in society as classes or other social strata. Those can be seen as (a) existing as some form of physical reality or (b) merely as mental concepts that produce certain patterns of conduct. To deal with society as objective reality and as an integrated structural whole is to regard it as a system, and as a consequence, one must then regard the individual as a function of the system, as Durkheim did. Simmel does not see it that way. To him, social structure is an assembly of social constructions.

Stranger   The person who represents an unknown culture and country and who is usually welcomed and even protected under strict rules of hospitality. Simmel sees him not as a person representing strangeness, but as a participant in a *strange relationship*.

Universalism   A system of ethics that emphasizes brotherly closeness among all humans (See also **Exclusivity**).

Western civilization   Civilization that developed around the Mediterranean in ancient Greece and the Roman Empire as a synthesis of Greek philosophy and religious ideas from Judaism, Christianity, and Islam. Its path through history led from antiquity via the Renaissance, the Reformation, and the Enlightenment to modern natural sciences, the Industrial Revolution, and political ideas of Marxism and democracy. Its regional identity has shifted from the countries around the Mediterranean to include all of Europe, North America, and South America.

References

Bargatzky, T. (1978). *Die Rolle des Fremden beim Kulturwandel.* Hamburg and Hohenschäftlarn: Renner.

Becher, H. (1984). Georg Simmel in Straßburg. *Sociologia Internationalis, 22*(5), 3–17.

Beck, U., & Grande, E. (2010). Varieties of second modernity: The cosmopolitan turn in social and political theory and research. *The British Journal of Sociology, 61*(3), 409–443.

Berger, P. L., & Luckmann, T. (1966). *The social construction of reality. A treatise in the sociology of knowledge.* Garden City, NY: Doubleday.

Blasi, A. J. (2010, March–April). *Georg Simmel's sociology of the family.* Paper presented at the annual meeting of the Midwest Sociological Society.

Comte, A. (1842). *Cours de philosophie positive* (Vol. 6). Paris: Lagrange.

Coser, L. (1968). Georg Simmel's style of work: A contribution to the sociology of the sociologist. *American Journal of Sociology, 63,* 635–641.

Darwin, C. (1859). *The origin of species by means of natural selection.* London: John Murray.

Draghici, S. (2001). *Georg Simmel, the pauper.* Washington, DC: Plutarch Press.

Durkheim, É. (1912). *Les formes elementaires de la vie religieuse: Le systeme totemique en Australie.* Paris: Alcan.

Durkheim, É. (1984). *The division of labor in society.* New York: The Free Press. (Original work published 1893)

Durkheim, É. (1995). *The elementary forms of religious life* (K. E. Fields, Trans.). New York: Free Press. (Original work published 1912)

Eisenstadt, S. N. (2000). Multiple realities. *Daedalus, 129*(1), 1–29.

Gassen, K., & Landmann, M. C. (1958). *Buch des Dankes an Georg Simmel.* Berlin: Duncker & Humblot.

Goffman, E. (1974). *Frame analysis. An essay on the organization of experience.* Cambridge, MA: Harvard University Press.

Graham, D. W. (2011). Heraclitus. In E. N. Zalta (Ed.), *The Stanford encyclopedia of philosophy* (Summer 2012 ed.). Retrieved from http://plato.stanford.edu/archives/sum2011/entries/heraclitus/

Haag, A. (2011). *Versuch über die moderne Seele Chinas. Eindrücke einer Psychoanalytikerin.* Giessen: Psychosozial-Verlag.

Harrington A., & Kemple T. M., (Eds.). (2012). Simmel's Sociological Metaphysics [Special double issue]. *Theory, Culture & Society, 29*(4), 6–25, 263–278.

Helle, H. J. (2000). Similarities in the work of Simmel and Znaniecki. In E. Halas (Ed.), *Florian Znaniecki's sociological theory and the challenges of the 21st century* (pp. 149–160). Frankfurt: Peter Lang.

Helle, H. J. (2013). *Messages from Georg Simmel.* Leiden and Boston: Brill.

James, W. (1901–1902). *The varieties of religious experience: A study in human nature.* Retrieved from http://www.worldu.edu/library/william_james_var.pdf

Kemple, T. (2007). Special section on Simmel's metaphysics, ethics, and aesthetics. *Theory, Culture & Society (Annual Review), 24*(7–8), 20–90.

Kemple, T. (2009). Weber/Simmel/Du Bois: Musical thirds of classical sociology. *Journal of Classical Sociology, 9*(2), 183–203.

Kemple, T. (2010). Thomas Kemple introduces "David Frisby on Georg Simmel and social theory." *Theory, Culture & Society.* Retrieved from http://theory cult. culturesociety.blogspot.ca/2010/12/photo-david-frisby-in-commemoration-of .html

Kraut, R. (2012). Plato. In E. N. Zalta (Ed.), *The Stanford encyclopedia of philosophy* (Summer 2012 ed.). Retrieved from http://plato.stanford.edu/archives/sum2012/ entries/plato

Levine, D. N., Carter, E. B., & Mills Gorman, E. (1976). Simmel's influence on American sociology. *American Journal of Sociology, 81,* 1112–1132.

Marx, K. (1985). Contribution to the critique of Hegel's philosophy of law: Introduction. In K. Marx & F. Engels (Eds.), *On religion* (pp. 38–52). Moscow: Progress. (Original work published 1844)

Mead, G. H. (1901). [Review of the book *Philosophie des Geldes,* by Georg Simmel]. *Journal of Political Economy, 9,* 616–619.

Nelson, B. (1969). *The idea of usury: From tribal brotherhood to universal otherhood* (2nd ed.). Chicago and London: University of Chicago Press.

Park, R. E. (1928). Human migration and the marginal man. *American Journal of Sociology, 33,* 881–893.

Raushenbush, W. (1979). *Robert E. Park: Biography of a sociologist. With a foreword and epilogue by Everett C. Hughes.* Durham, NC: Duke University Press.

Riesman, D. (2001). *The lonely crowd.* New Haven, CT and London: Yale University Press. (Original work published 1950)

Schnabel, P.-E. (1976). Georg Simmel. In D. Käsler (Ed.), *Klassiker des soziologischen Denkens* (pp. 267–311). München: C. H. Beck.

Shen, G. (2001). *Chinese small town.* Aldershot, Hampshire, UK: Ashgate.

Shibutani, T. (1955). Reference groups as perspectives. *American Journal of Sociology, 60,* 562–569.

Simmel, G. (1881). *Das Wesen der Materie nach Kants Physischer Monadologie.* Inaugural Dissertation zur Erlangung der Doctorwürde von der Philosophischen Fakultät der Friedrich-Wilhelms-Universität zu Berlin genehmigt und Freitag den 25. Februar 1881 öffentlich verteidigt. (Doctoral dissertation, University of Berlin, Berlin, Germany).

Simmel, G. (1882). Psychologische und ethnologische Studien über Musik [Studies in psychology and cultural anthropology of music]. *Zeitschrift für Völkerpsychologie und Sprachwissenschaft, 13,* 261–305.

Simmel, G. (1890a). *Über sociale Differenzierung. Sociologische und psychologische Untersuchungen.* Leipzig: Duncker & Humblot.

Simmel, G. (1890b). Zur Psychologie der Frauen. In M. Lazarus & H. Steinthal (Eds.), *Zeitschrift für Völkerpsychologie und Sprachwissenschaft* (Vol. 20, pp. 6–46). Berlin: Ferd. Dümmler.

Simmel, G. (1892). *Einleitung in die Moralwissenschaft. Eine Kritik der ethischen Grundbegriffe* (Vol. 1). Berlin: Hertz.

Simmel, G. (1893). *Einleitung in die Moralwissenschaft. Eine Kritik der ethischen Grundbegriffe* (Vol. 2). Berlin: Hertz.

Simmel, G. (1895a). The problem of sociology. *Annals of the American Academy of Political and Social Science, 6*(3), 412–423.

Simmel, G. (1895b). Zur Soziologie der Familie. *Vossische Zeitung,* Sonntagsbeilagen 26–27.

Simmel, G. (1903a). Die Großstädte und das Geistesleben. In *Vorträge und Aufsätze zur Städteausstellung: Jahrbuch der Gehe-Stiftung zu Dresden* (Vol. IX, pp. 185–206). Dresden: Gehe-Stiftung.

Simmel, G. (1903b). Soziologie der Konkurrenz. *Neue Deutsche Rundschau, 14,* 1009–1023.

Simmel, G. (1905). *Die Probleme der Geschichtsphilosophie. Eine erkenntnistheoretische Studie* (2nd ed.). Leipzig: Duncker & Humblot.

Simmel, G. (1906). Kant und Goethe [pamphlet]. In *Die Kultur* (Vol. 10). Berlin: Bard, Marquardt & Co.

Simmel, G. (1907). *Philosophie des Geldes* (2nd ed.). Leipzig: Duncker & Humblot.

Simmel, G. (1908a). *Soziologie. Untersuchungen über die Formen der Vergesellschaftung.* Leipzig: Duncker & Humblot.

Simmel, G. (1908b). Exkurs über den Fremden. In G. Simmel (Ed.), *Soziologie: Untersuchungen über die Formen der Vergesellschaftung* (pp. 685–691). Leipzig: Duncker & Humblot.

Simmel, G. (1913). *Goethe.* Leipzig: Klinckhardt & Biermann.

Simmel, G. (1916). *Kant und Goethe: Zur Geschichte der modernen Weltanschauung* (3rd ed.). Leipzig: Kurt Wolff.

Simmel, G. (1918). *Lebensanschauung. Vier metaphysische Kapitel.* München und Leipzig: Duncker & Humblot.

Simmel, G. (1919). *Rembrandt: Ein kunstphilosophischer Versuch* (2nd ed.). Leipzig: Kurt Wolff. (Original work published 1916)

Simmel, G. (1922). *Philosophie des Geldes* (4th ed.). München and Leipzig: Duncker & Humblot.

Simmel, G. (1924). *Kant: Sechzehn Vorlesungen, gehalten an der Berliner Universität* (6th ed.). Leipzig: Duncker & Humblot. (Original work published 1904)

Simmel, G. (1949). Ethik und Probleme der modernen Kultur. Vorlesung 1913. Nachschrift von Kurt Gassen. *Philosophische Studien, 1,* 310–344.

Simmel, G. (1950). The metropolis and mental life. In K. Wolff (Trans.), *The Sociology of Georg Simmel* (pp. 409–424). New York: Free Press.

Simmel, G. (1955). *Conflict & The web of group-affiliations* (K. H. Wolff & R. Bendix, Trans.). Glencoe, IL: The Free Press.

Simmel, G. (1977). *The problems of the philosophy of history: An epistemological essay* (G. Oakes, Ed. & Trans.). New York: The Free Press.

Simmel, G. (1980). *Essays on interpretation in social science* (G. Oakes, Ed. & Trans.). Totowa, NJ: Rowman and Littlefield.

Simmel, G. (1997). *Essays on religion.* New Haven, CT and London: Yale University Press.

Simmel, G. (2009). *Sociology: Inquiries into the construction of social forms* (2 Vols.). Leiden and Boston: Brill. (Original work published 1908)

Smelser, N. J. (1995). *Problematics of sociology: The Georg Simmel lectures.* Berkeley: University of California Press.

Strauss, A. L. (1959). *Mirrors and masks: The search for identity.* Glencoe, IL: The Free Press.

Tenbruck, F. (1958). Georg Simmel (1858–1918). *Kölner Zeitschrift für Soziologie und Sozialpsychologie, 10,* 587–614.

Üner, E. (1992). *Soziologie als "geistige Bewegung": Hans Freyers System der Soziologie und die "Leipziger Schule."* München: Oldenbourg Akademieverlag.

von Wiese, L. (1910). Neuere soziologische Literatur. *Archiv für Sozialwissenschaft und Sozialpolitik, XXXI,* 882–907.

Weber, M. (1920). Die protestantische Ethik und der Geist des Kapitalismus. In *Gesammelte Aufsätze zur Religionssoziologie* (S. 17–206). Tübingen: J. B. C. Mohr (P. Siebeck). (Original work published 1904)

Weber, M. (1951). Roscher und Knies und die logischen Probleme der historischen Nationalökonomie II. Knies und das Irrationalitätsproblem. In *Gesammelte Aufsätze zur Wissenschaftslehre* (S. 42–105). Tübingen: J. B. C. Mohr (P. Siebeck). (Original work published 1905)

Weber, M. (2013). *Economy and society.* Berkeley: University of California Press. (Original work published 1920)

Weinstein, D. (n.d.). *The metropolis and mental life by Georg Simmel.* Retrieved from http://condor.depaul.edu/dweinste/theory/M&ML.htm

Zank, M. (2008). Martin Buber. In E. N. Zalta (Ed.), *The Stanford encyclopedia of philosophy* (Fall 2008 ed.). Retrieved from http://plato.stanford.edu/archives/fall2008/entries/buber/

Index

About the Author

Horst J. Helle is a native and resident of Germany. He has an MBA from the University of Kansas. Before and after his graduate work there, he studied at the university in his hometown of Hamburg. There he received another business degree, a doctorate of philosophy in sociology, and the license to teach sociology as *Privatdozent*. Then he held tenured professorships at the Aachen Institute of Technology, the University of Vienna, and the University of Munich. Throughout his career he has worked in other countries, including spending a year as a research fellow at The University of Chicago and, since 1996, teaching in mainland China. For additional information and a list of his publications, see http://www.horst-helle.de.

⑤SAGE research**methods**

The essential online tool for researchers from the world's leading methods publisher

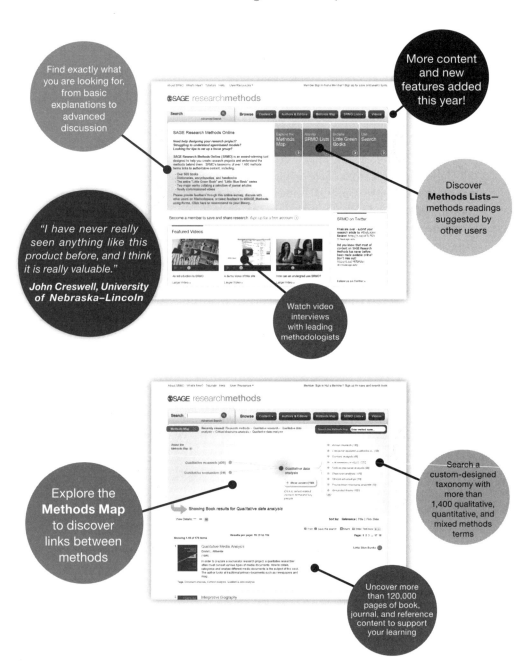

Find exactly what you are looking for, from basic explanations to advanced discussion

More content and new features added this year!

Discover **Methods Lists**— methods readings suggested by other users

"I have never really seen anything like this product before, and I think it is really valuable."

John Creswell, University of Nebraska–Lincoln

Watch video interviews with leading methodologists

Explore the **Methods Map** to discover links between methods

Search a custom-designed taxonomy with more than 1,400 qualitative, quantitative, and mixed methods terms

Uncover more than 120,000 pages of book, journal, and reference content to support your learning

Find out more at
www.sageresearchmethods.com